# Cracking the Code:
## The Confused Traveler's Guide to Liberian English

By John-Mark Sheppard

Cover photo and art by Heidi Sheppard

jms-book@sheppardsmissions.org

Published by Sheppard's Books, USA

Non-fiction
1.   English Dictionaries – Liberian English
2.   Liberian Languages – Liberian English

ISBN: 978-0-9832640-3-3

Sheppard, John Mark, 1982-

**Dedication:**

For Sara, the love of my life. Thank you for support
and patience as I kept saying, "It's almost done."

See? It's done!

# Introduction

Many a Westerner who first finds he will be working in Liberia is thrilled to learn English is the official language of the country. Rather than toiling with a tongue-twisting language such as French, Swahili or Amharic, our traveler looks forward to instant communication in his mother tongue. However, shortly after being hit with an overpowering blast of heat and humidity as he steps off the climate-controlled plane, he is struck by an even more startling reality; he can understand almost nothing of the language being spoken around him! "Are they even speaking English?" he asks himself incredulously.

As he settles into his new home our traveler grows more familiar with the Liberian accent and starts to pick up words here and there, but there are many words he has never before heard. And many words he does recognize are used in incomprehensible ways. As he settles in to his new role he wonders why it is that Liberians do not speak "real English." He may even make it his mission to correct the speech of everyone around him. This of course has little effect other than alienating would-be friends. Rather than truly getting to know the very people he came to work with, he retreats into the safety of the ex-pat "ghetto" where everyone speaks like he does.

Is there another alternative? Is it possible to truly understand and communicate in Liberian English without spending decades in the country? It most certainly is! If you have ever wondered why Liberian English is the way it is, and have wanted to "crack the code," this book is for you. It has often been said that you can never truly understand a culture until you speak the language. Those who take the time to learn to understand and even speak Liberian English find it to be a rich medium of communication. They are able to build strong friendships and understand Liberian culture at a deeper level then they ever thought possible.

## My Story

I personally have been greatly enriched by the relationships I have had with Liberians throughout the years. As the son of missionaries to Liberia, I was first exposed to Liberian English at the tender age of three. Some of my earliest memories are from the mission station where my family lived in Nimba County. There as I explored with my friends, the sounds and cadence of Liberian English became forever imprinted in my mind. When civil war broke out in Liberia my family moved to Côte d'Ivoire to help the Liberian refugees living across the border. Although we would travel to the United States every few years for furlough, the majority of my growing-up years were spent around Liberians.

Despite all the civil unrest going on around us, the memories of my childhood in Africa are overwhelmingly positive. Swinging from vines into rivers, raising a veritable menagerie of exotic pets, exploring the rainforest, and fishing in rivers and creeks with homemade poles alongside my Liberian friends are memories I will cherish forever.

Later, after graduating from college I returned to Liberia to work in the field of community development. By this time I had been away from Africa for several years and my Liberian English had grown rusty. I could see immediately that making a conscious effort to brush up on the language would have immense benefits. I began compiling a list of Liberian English words based on conversations with Liberian friends and acquaintances, scribbling new words in notebooks and odd scraps of paper as I went about my work. At the same time I worked on improving my accent. Foreigners wanted to know how I was able to speak like that – how I was able to "crack the code."

That wordlist became the core of this dictionary. In my neverending quest for new words for this project, I made use of several long out of print resources. I am heavily indebted to Warren d'Azevedo's 1967 work "Some Terms from Liberian Speech" which was revised and expanded by Michael Gold in 1997. NYU professor John Singler also published numerous papers on Liberian English that have proved to be helpful references.

Liberian English is constantly evolving and many words in these pre-civil war works are no longer widely used, and thus were not included in the dictionary. Many new words have also entered the Liberian vocabulary. Liberian English is entering the information age and many Liberians are using such online media as Facebook and Internet forums to communicate. I was able to find many new words through these websites. Any unfamiliar words gleaned from these sources were verified with Liberian colleagues. To my friends like Ansu Konneh, Koffa Swen and especially Jackson Gbah, who helped me in this work, I owe a debt of gratitude.

# A Brief History of English in Liberia

Common wisdom has it that freed slaves from the United States first introduced the English language to Liberia. Indeed the English spoken in Liberia more closely resembles American English than do the other English-based creoles spoken in the former British colonies of West Africa. However, careful historical research shows that English was spoken in the region that is today Liberia long before the first American settlers arrived in 1821.

In the 15th century the Portuguese began exploring West Africa for the purpose of trade. Other European traders followed in the 17th century, including the Dutch and the British. Europeans knew what is today the Republic of Liberia as the "Pepper Coast" because of the abundance of melegueta pepper. Spices were in high demand at the time, along with slaves who were needed to work the plantations of the New World colonies. Intertribal warfare along the Pepper Coast provided a steady stream of human cargo for the transatlantic slave trade and, sadly, slaves were exported even after Liberia was formed as a republic and slavery was officially banned.

By the time the African-American settlers arrived in Liberia the British had been actively trading along the Pepper Coast for over 150 years. The first settlers found a large number of indigenous people who had already learned English through trading contacts with the British. A white missionary named Jehudi Ashmun who oversaw the activities of the early settlers remarked, "Very many in all the maritime tribes, speak a corruption of the English language."[1]

This "corruption of the English language" referred to by Ashmun is known today by

> ## Kru Pidgin English
> Born on British merchant vessels during the colonial era, Kru Pidgin English was spoken as a second language by many until recently in Grand Kru County. Men from the coastal Klao and Grebo tribes, known collectively as the "Kru", were hired by the British to work in their colonies in West Africa, and even as far as the Caribbean and Central America. Today Kru Pidgin English is only spoken by a handful of elderly people, as this dialect has been largely replaced among the younger generations by Liberian Vernacular English. It shares many features in common with the Krio spoken in Sierra Leone.

---

[1] African Repository, Nov. 1827:263

scholars as West African Pidgin English. A pidgin is differentiated from a creole language in that a pidgin has no mother-tongue speakers. Being a basic version of English with a simplified grammar and limited vocabulary, Pidgin English was easily learned as a second language by African traders and deck hands on British vessels. In Liberia, this form of English was developed by coastal Kwa-speaking African sailors and became known as <u>Kru Pidgin English</u>. Related pidgins became widespread in West Africa especially in the British colonies of The Gambia, Sierra Leone, Ghana and Nigeria.

The freed slaves who founded the republic of Liberia brought with them other forms of English. The goal of the early Americo-Liberian leaders was to populate their new republic with educated blacks from the U.S. who spoke Standard English. The elite ruling class was made up of people with a mixed racial heritage, many of whom had received a university education. Like the Europeans of the 1800s, the Americo-Liberians sought to subdue the peoples of the African interior with the colonial trinity of civilization, commerce and Christianity. Essential to all of this was the adoption of the English language. In the settlers' minds, their possession of the English language elevated them above the "savage" tribes of their new land. One Rev. Alexander Crummell remarked in an oration given on Liberia's independence day in 1860,

> ### Settler English
> Also known as "Congo English," this dialect is spoken by the descendants of the freed slaves who founded the Republic of Liberia. Settler English can be heard today mainly in isolated upriver settlements in Sinoe County. The dialect has little influence on the non-settler population, and some aspects of Settler English are stigmatized by speakers of Liberian Vernacular English.

> [T]he exile of our fathers from their African homes to America, had given us, their children, at least one item of compensation, namely, the possession of the Anglo-Saxon tongue; that this language put us in a position which none other on the globe could give us; and that it was impossible to estimate too highly; the prerogatives and the elevation the Almighty has bestowed upon us, in our having as our own speech, the speech of Chaucer and Shakespeare, of Milton and Wordsworth, of Bacon and Burke, or Franklin and Webster.[2]

---

[2] Crummel, Alexander. The Future of Africa. 1862: 9

Despite their lofty ideals, the high mortality rate among the settlers and the precarious nature of the whole Liberian enterprise meant the American Colonization Society would have great difficulty recruiting emigrants for Liberia. Many of the former slaves who did emigrate had received little or no education and spoke the creolized English used by slaves on rural southern plantations, remembered today in North America through the stories of Uncle Ramus and Brer Rabbit. This form of English has been preserved in Liberia in what is known as <u>Settler English</u>, and can still be heard in some upriver communities of Sinoe County.

Until Samuel Doe's overthrow of President Tolbert's regime in 1980 the Americo-Liberians maintained a monopoly of power over Liberia. Although making up fewer than 5% of the population, the decedents of the settlers held all the key government positions. Beyond their political dominance, the cultural and linguistic influence of the Americo-Liberians cannot be underestimated. Tribal languages were denigrated as "dialects" and very few settlers attempted to learn or study them. In a Liberia dominated by an English-speaking elite, a man could not hold on to his tribal identify if he wished to succeed in society. Many tribal families sent their children to live as wards in the homes of Americo-Liberians. These children worked as servants while receiving an education and learning the English language. Many other members of the indigenous population found alternate means of learning English, adopted a "Christian" name, and modified their identities in an effort to become *kwi* (civilized.) Even today in urban centers such as Monrovia, people from the interior who choose to speak their mother tongue in a public setting are often stigmatized.

Near the beginning the 20th century the Liberian government began to bring the numerous tribes of the interior under their control. Their primary means of doing so was through the establishment of the Liberian Frontier Force, the original Armed Forces of Liberia (AFL). In 1926 the Firestone Rubber Company came to Liberia. Both the Frontier Force and Firestone required large amounts of labor. Many men from the Lorma and related Mande-speaking ethnic groups from northern Liberia began to fill Frontier Force positions. A common language was need to facilate communication with other recruits, Firestone employees, and the population of the interior. As a result, another form of pidgin English developed, commonly known as *Firestone English* or *Soldier English*.[3] *Soldier English* combined Liberian Settler English with certain aspects the Mande languages spoken by

---

[3] Kortmann et all. <u>A Handbook of Varieties of English A Multimedia Reference Tool. Volume 1: Phonology.</u> Mouton de Gruyter. 2004, 875

the soldiers and plantation workers. It spread throughout Liberia as the Frontier Force established Liberian control over the interior through such measures as the hated "hut tax."[4] Firestone plantation workers, returning to their home villages, also were influential in the spread of this new language. Eventually this variety, known academically as "Liberian Interior Pidgin English," became the *lingua franca* of the Liberian interior.

By far the most common form of English in Liberia today is Liberian Vernacular English. Liberian Vernacular English appears to have developed as a result of the contact between Settler English and Interior Pidgin English speakers in the Monrovia area. As a result of the civil war and the massive displacement of the Liberian population, Liberian Vernacular English became the *de facto* language of wider communication among Liberians.

# Attitudes Towards English in Liberia

Although many tribal languages are spoken in Liberia, English is the official language and by far the most dominant. It is the language of the classroom, marketplace, government, and increasingly, the home. In Liberia when two people of different ethnic groups marry, they typically use Liberian Vernacular English to communicate in the home. Thus many children learn Liberian English as their mother tongue. Today in some tribal communities, especially those along the coast, the native language is being replaced by Liberian English. Parents fail to teach their children their mother tongue as it is seen as having neither prestige nor economic value.

Liberians take great pride in their knowledge of the English language. While other English-based creoles of West African counties are known locally as *Pidgin* or *Krio*, Liberians generally refer to all the varieties spoken in their country as simply "English." Some speakers of Liberian Vernacular English will, however, refer to their speech as *English* or *Clear English*, differentiating it from varieties such as *Sirees*, the Liberian word for American English. Those who have recognized the distinctiveness of Liberian Vernacular English have developed a number of colorful terms for this language including *Waterside English*, *Potato Greens English* and *Colloqua*.

---

[4] The hut tax was a measure by the Liberian government to generate revenue by taxing each household, with little or no benefits ever seen for those being taxed.

Linguists studying creole languages recognize in speakers a continuum between those whose speech most closely resembles the official variety of the language (i.e. Standard English) and those whose speech is farthest from it. The dialect closest to the source language is known as the acrolect, while the furthest is known as the basilect. In the middle is the mesolect, which is spoken by the majority of the population. In Liberia, Liberian Standard English is the acrolect while Liberian Vernacular English is the mesolect. It should be remembered that even among mesolectical speakers of Liberian Vernacular English, pronunciation and grammar can vary significantly. This book is an attempt to point out widespread patterns of speech in Liberian Vernacular English, but bear in mind variations are likely to be heard.

Liberian attitudes towards non-standard forms of English vary significantly. Many people of the educated class who are aware of the distinctiveness of the local dialect tend to regard Liberian Vernacular English with a sense of amusement or even embarrassment. On the grassroots level, however, there seems to be an awareness of the limitations of using Standard English in Liberia. There is now a growing acceptance of Liberian English as a legitimate means of communication. A pioneer in this area was the novelist Bai T. Moore, whose works such as *Murder in the Cassava Patch* and *The Money Doubler* make extensive use of Liberian colloquial in the characters' dialogue. Newspapers now regularly print cartoons in Liberian English and many NGOs have taken to producing educational posters in this language. In recent years there has been an increasing amount of audio and visual media being produced in Liberian Vernacular English.

Radio stations such as Star Radio have begun to produce dramas and news broadcasts in language easily understood by the man on the street. Even the current president of Liberia, Ellen Johnson-Sirleaf has taken to addressing the nation over radio in "Simple English."[5] The Malawala Balawala drama company has paved the way for Liberian Vernacular English visual media by producing short comedies and informational films in Liberian Vernacular English since the mid 1980s. Today other small companies are beginning to produce longer films in Liberian English, cashing in on the popularity of Nigeria's "Nollywood" soap operas. The burgeoning music industry in Liberia is another means by which Liberian Vernacular English is gaining public recognition and acceptance. "Hip-co" artists like Luckay

---

[5] The broadcast language called "Simple English" differs slightly from LVE. It uses a very limited English vocabulary and omits common words in LVE borrowed from native languages.

Buckay and JD Donzo combine hip-hop rhythms with Liberian street slang and are immensely popular with Liberian youth.

The history of English in Liberia is rich and varied. From its beginnings as a coastal pidgin to the dominating influence of Americo-Liberian settlers, Liberian Vernacular English has developed into a vibrant creole. While once only spoken on the street and in the home, Liberian Vernacular English can now be heard on the radio and television and seen in newspapers, proving it to be a force to be reckoned with.

# Advice for Westerners in Liberia

Liberian Vernacular English and Standard English are only minimally mutually intelligible. However, many Liberians can understand Standard English fairly well, even if they cannot speak it. This is especially true of those in urban areas who have been educated and listen to Standard English radio broadcasting on the BBC and other stations. This means that initially Westerners will probably be understood better by the Liberians than visa versa. However, unless the newcomer learns to reproduce the dialect, or at least alter his choice of words, much of what he says will be lost to children and those from rural areas with less exposure to Standard English. Western speakers of Standard English should work to master common words and expressions used in Liberian English. Even without significantly altering one's accent, Westerners can be better understood by using appropriate word choices. For example, while "pants" and "trousers" are basically synonymous in Standard English, the word "pants" is almost never used in Liberia.

Eventually many Westerners come to understand Liberian Vernacular English very well and some even learn to speak it fluently. While there can be great benefits to this, speaking the language should be approached with care. In certain situations Liberians may be very pleased to hear a Westerner speaking Liberian English. However, in other instances it may come across as being condescending or insulting. As a general rule, the more formal a situation and the more educated the person with whom one is speaking, the more one's speech should conform to Standard English. While it would be perfectly acceptable to use Liberian Vernacular English to buy produce from a market woman, a government official would likely feel as if a Westerner was talking down to him for doing the same thing. In a phenomena known by linguists as code-switching, Liberians themselves often adapt their speech according to the situation. Most will speak to Westerners in their "best" English, and expect the same back –until perhaps a friendship is established or close sense of familiarity develops.

# Liberia's Indigenous People and Languages

Most published accounts of Liberia's history begin in the 1800s with an almost exclusive focus given to the nation-building efforts of the Americo-Liberians. Scant attention is given to the histories of the indigenous peoples. However, for a fuller understanding of the state of English in Liberia today, it is necessary to briefly explore Liberia's indigenous ethnic groups.

The government of Liberia officially recognizes 16 indigenous groups called "tribes." Linguists who have conducted surveys in Liberia however have identified as many as thirty distinct ethnolinguistic groups. The government's classification for the most part was done in the mid to late 20th century as a means of consolidating power. In some cases, such as for the Kru and Grebo, a number of ethnic groups sharing neither a sense of solidarity or even mutually intelligible languages were considered to be the same "tribe" merely because of geographic proximity and presumed common ancestry.

The history of human habitation in what is today the Republic of Liberia is relatively recent, probably dating back no more than seven or eight hundred years. The earliest inhabitants are generally agreed to be the Dey people of the Kwa language groups. The Kwa speaking ethnic groups trace their origins to eastern Africa. Evidence of their migration can be found in related ethnic groups stretching as far east as Nigeria. The Kwa settled in Liberia along the coast in several waves and eventually divided into the Bassa, Grebo, Belle, Krahn, Gbi and Kru ethnic groups. Shortly after the Dey settled in Liberia, the Atlantic-speaking Gola arrived from the north and established powerful chiefdoms in the northwest region.

Southwest Mande speaking groups such as the Kpelle, Lorma and Bandi arrived in Liberia in the 1500s and pushed the Gola southward towards the coast. These groups trace their origins to the savannas of what is today the Republic of Guinea, and themselves were probably driven southward by the increasingly powerful Manding peoples of Guinea and Mali. Numerous wars were fought in the savanna and forest regions from the 1600s to the early 1900s by Manding warlords seeking to solidify control over trade routes, capture slaves and convert "pagans" to Islam. Many animistic groups, such as Atlantic-speaking Kissi and the Southeast Mande-speaking Mano and Gio ethnic groups, apparently sought refuge from the turmoil of the savannas in the forests of modern Liberia and established themselves there.

The Vai represent an early Manding group in Liberia who settled among the Gola in the 15th century as salt, kola and slave traders.[6] The Mandingo have been present in Liberia for many hundreds of years, usually living as minority traders, blacksmiths and Islamic clerics among other ethnic groups, although many homogeneous Mandingo settlements can be found today in Lofa County. Despite their long history in the country, many other ethnic groups regard the Mandingo as outsiders.

## Approximate Boundaries of Liberia's Officially Recognized Ethnic Groups

---

[6] Person, Yves. "Review: Ethnic Movements and Acculturation in Upper Guinea since the Fifteenth Century." <u>African Historical Studies,</u> Vol. 4, No. 3 (1971.) Boston University African Studies Center, 676

## Liberian Language Family Tree

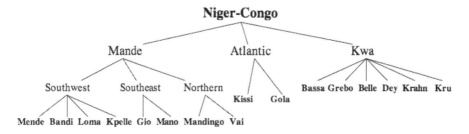

**Niger-Congo**

Mande     Atlantic     Kwa

Southwest   Southeast   Northern    Kissi   Gola    Bassa Grebo Belle Dey Krahn Kru

Mende Bandi Loma Kpelle Gio Mano Mandingo Vai

# Features of Liberian English

The indigenous languages have had a profound impact on how English is spoken in Liberia. Liberian Vernacular English had its origins as a pidgin, but today it could be properly considered a creole language in that it has become the mother tongue of many Liberians. For the formation of a creole, two languages are necessary: the lexifier language and the substrate language. The lexifier language is that which gives the creole the majority of its words, while the underlying substrate language provides the grammatical "skeleton" which gives the rules for the words to function. The substrate language also heavily influences the pronunciation of the creole. The unique pronunciation and grammatical features of Liberian English can be traced to the indigenous substrate languages, especially Mande languages such as Kpelle, Lorma, Vai and Mandingo.

## Pronunciation

Linguists refer to the study of how the sounds of a language interact with each other as phonology. Liberian Vernacular English has a uniquely African phonology which can be traced to the Niger-Congo substrate languages. Below is an explanation of the language's rules of pronunciation followed by a brief grammar sketch.

The consonant and vowels of Liberian English are very similar to those of American English. There are, however, several sounds present in Liberian Vernacular English borrowed from the indigenous languages that are not found in American English. These can be heard in place names, borrowed words and personal names. The most common of these are the "gb" and "ny" sound. "Gb" is produced by articulating [g] and [b] simultaneously. The palatalized "ny" [ɲ] sound is used in Standard English in words such as "onion" where it only occurs between vowels. In Liberian English, however, this sound is

11

common at the beginning of syllables. Below is a summary of Liberian Vernacular English sounds using the International Phonetic Alphabet (IPA) with corresponding examples from either American English (or Liberian Vernacular English when the sound is unique to this language.)

<u>Consonants</u>

| *Stops*: | *Double Articulated Stops:* |
|---|---|
| b as in "<u>b</u>oat" | g͡b as in "<u>gb</u>alan" (Liberian Vernacula English: "weapon") |
| p as in "<u>p</u>ot" | |
| d as in "<u>d</u>og" | k͡p as in "<u>Kp</u>elle" (Liberian ethnic group) |
| t as in "<u>t</u>op" | *Semivowels*: |
| g as in "<u>g</u>oat" | j as in "<u>y</u>ear" |
| k as in "<u>c</u>ap" | w as in "<u>w</u>ar" |
| *Nasals*: | *Sibilants*: |
| n as in "<u>n</u>ap" | s as in "<u>s</u>ap" |
| m as in "<u>m</u>an" | z as in "<u>z</u>oo" |
| ŋ as in "ri<u>ng</u>" | ʃ as in "<u>sh</u>op" |
| ɲ as in "Ke<u>ny</u>a" | ʒ as in "sei<u>z</u>ure" |
| *Affricates*: | *Liquids*: |
| t͡ʃ as in "<u>ch</u>op" | l as in "<u>l</u>eap" |
| d͡ʒ as in "<u>j</u>am" | r as in "<u>r</u>at" |

<u>Vowels</u>

| | | *Glides*: |
|---|---|---|
| o as in "<u>o</u>pen" | u as in "sch<u>oo</u>l" | ai as in "<u>i</u>rony" |
| ɔ as in "<u>aw</u>ful" | ʊ as in "t<u>oo</u>k" | au as in "c<u>ow</u>" |
| e as in "<u>a</u>pe" | ʌ as in "c<u>u</u>p" | ɔɪ as in "b<u>oy</u>" |
| ε as in "r<u>e</u>nt" | ə as in "t<u>u</u>mble" | |
| i as in "h<u>ea</u>t" | a as in "d<u>o</u>t" | |
| ɪ as in "h<u>i</u>p" | æ as in "c<u>a</u>t" | |

# Phonology

## Open Syllables:

Liberian English is most notable for the way the endings are dropped off of many words. A common misconception by many Westerns is that this is due to laziness or sloppy speech. This is not the case. The reason they are not pronounced is because the speakers are simply following the sound patterns of the native Niger-Congo languages. So for example, "dog" is usually pronounced [dɔ]. Liberian languages are comprised of words made from open syllables (i.e. a single consonant followed by a vowel). All evidence points to the fact that consonant endings are underlying in Liberian Vernacular English. For example the word "cut" is realized as [kʌ], while "cutting" is pronounced [kʌfi]. Coda consonants are often pronounced when they are followed by a word starting with vowel. For example, "bring it" would be pronounced [bɹĩ kɪ].

## Syllable Simplification:

Liberian English does not favor consonant clusters, especially in the syllable final position. This tendency to simplify consonant clusters means that, for example, in words ending in [pt] only the [p] will remain in the final pronunciation. In consonant clusters ending in a sibilant such as [ks], the stop is dropped and the [s] is retained. So, the Standard English verb "fix" [fɪkʰs] is pronounced [fɪs] in Liberian Vernacular English. Silabants are also retained in plural nouns such as "beans" [bĩs]. For syllables ending with a stop [t, d, p, b, k, g] such a *fut* "full, overflowing," the consonant is unreleased (meaning it is not aspirated as in Standard English).[7]

## Vowel Lengthening:

The rules of pronunciation in Liberian English which lead to the dropping of certain consonants also affect many vowels. This is true of the liquids [r] and [l]. Rather than pronouncing the final [r], the preceding vowel is lengthened. For example "car" is pronounced [ka:]. The liquid [l] behaves in the same way.

---

[7] Singler, John. "There was fly before dog ear get [a] sore: Vernacular Liberian English vis-à-vis early African American English and still earlier West African Pidgin English." Symposium in honor of David Dwyer, Michigan State University. 2006, 6

## Nasalization:

Syllables ending with a nasal in Standard English are modified by dropping the consonant and nasalizing the vowel, which means some words may only be distinguished by the nasalization of a vowel. For instance, "reed" and "ring" are pronounced [ɹi] and [ɹĩ] respectively. Finally, there is a tendency to simplify diphthongs by dropping the second vowel. So for instance the word "time" is often pronounced [tã]. The simplification of word endings means that often words that are not homophones in Standard English become so in Liberian Vernacular English. For example, "Ed," "egg," and "air" are all pronounced [ɛ].

## Voicing Changes:

Another feature of Liberian English is that voiced consonants (those produced by vibrating the vocal cords) often become voiceless when they occur between vowels or in coda position. For instance, the [g] is replaced with [k] in *flok* (to beat).

## Weakening of Intervocalic Consonants:

Another strong tendency in Liberian English is the weakening of the consonants that occur between vowels. Thus the word "seven" is pronounced [sɛwɛ̃].

## Consonant Substitutions:

Liberian English also conforms to the Niger-Congo substrate languages in the way changes are made to Standard English consonants sounds. The most common examples of this are the dental fricatives or "th" sounds, which are produced by placing the tip of the tongue between the teeth. As these are not present in any of the Liberian languages, most speakers of Liberian English cannot pronounce them. How these sounds are substituted depends on their phonological environment. If they occur at the beginning of a word, usually the voiced "th" [ð] becomes a "d" while the voiceless "th" [θ] becomes a "t." For example, [dæ wa fi dɛ] "That's what thing there?" When [θ] occurs at the end of a word it is either pronounced as an [f] or a [t], so the word "truth" is pronounced [tɹuf], while the word "faith" becomes [fet]. When the voiced "th" [ð] occurs between vowels it becomes a [v] or [d] so "father" is pronounced [fada].

In the indigenous languages the [l], [r] and [d] sounds are often interchangeable. Likewise for many speakers of Liberian English use these consonants interchangably when they occur between vowels. For example "ready" may be pronounced [ɹɛli] and "problem" [pɹaɹɛ̃]. Some speakers of Liberian English whose mother tongue is a Southwest Mande language such as Lorma may substitute [l] for [r] at the beginning of a word (i.e. "load" might be pronounced [ɹo] –much to the amusement of other Liberians).

In the Niger-Congo languages the [nd] and [n] sounds are often interchangeable. Thus for example the name of the Mende [mɛnde] ethnic group may also be pronounced as [mẽne]. Likewise in Liberian Vernacular English, when a [d] is proceeded by a nasal, it is often assimilated to become a nasal. This is most often heard with the *dem* plural marker which often ends up sounding like [nẽ] as in *All dee ting nen* (All these thing them). "All these things." Finally, there is also an interesting tendency to switch the [sk] sounds and [st] consonant clusters. For example "screen" becomes "streen" and "stretch" is pronounced "skrech."

## A Note about Liberian English Orthography

There have been several attempts in the past to reduce Liberian Vernacular English to writing, but as of yet there is no officially accepted orthography. Spellings may vary widely in different publications. There is, however, at least one commonly accepted spelling convention used in Liberia. The letters "or" are used to represent the back near open vowel [ɔ]. The [r] is not pronounced. Hence, the name of the Lorma [lɔ:ma] ethnic group is often spelled "Lorma." This convention is retained in the orthography used in this book. It should be noted that Liberian English is an "r-less" language, meaning "r" is not pronounced at the end of syllables (similar to a New York accent.) However, for the sake of readability the "r" is generally left in the spelling. The "r" should not be pronounced but rather the preceding vowel should be lengthened. So for example *markeh* "market" should be pronounced [ma:kɛ].

Due to Liberian Vernacular English's tendency to drop the final consonants in words, some have placed the apostrophe mark (') in the place of the dropped letter. This method seemed rather unwieldy and unsatisfactory to me, so I adapted the orthography used in the Gullah "Nyew Testament" published for speakers of the related Gullah language, spoken by African-Americans living on the Sea Islands of South Carolina.

If there is no significant difference in the pronunciation of a word between Standard and Liberian English, the Standard English spelling is given. Otherwise a phonetic representation is given, with the Standard English spelling following in italics. Endings of words that are normally unpronounced in Liberian Vernacular English may be left on for the sake of clarity.

# Grammar Sketch: Noun Phrases

### Plurality:

For the most part nouns are only used in their singular form in Liberian Vernacular English. To indicate plurality, the pronoun *dem* "them" is added. For example, *Oreta cup dem on de* table. "Oretha's cups are on the table." Many of the native Niger-Congo languages make use of similar particles.

There are however, some words in Liberian English that were pidginized in their plural form. They are rarely if ever used in the singular. For example:

| | |
|---|---|
| aches – *ashes* | maches - *matches* |
| ans – *ants* | teet - *teeth* |
| beans - *beans* | |

Despite their already plural form, the word *dem* is often used on these nouns. e.g.

*De beans dem wase on de floor.*

The beans them waste on the floor.

"The beans spilled on the floor."

*Dem* can also function as an associative plural to mean "and the others" as in,

*A budduh wif Prince dem to de video club.*

I butt up with Prince them to the video club.

"I ran into Prince and the others at the video club."

## Determiners:

Liberian English makes use of the definite article "de," in the same way "the" is used in Standard English. However, the indefinite article "a" is generally not used. The sentence "Willy has a dog" would usually be rendered *Willy get dog.* However, the word *one* may also function as the definite article when specification is needed. For example,

*She get one big chicken to de hus.*

She get one big chicken to the house.

"She has a big chicken at her house."

## Pronouns:

The pronouns of Liberian English are largely the same as those for Standard English, although the pronunciation is different. One idiosyncrasy of the speech of many rural Liberians for whom Liberian English is a second or third language is their inability to differentiate gender specific pronouns. Thus, both "he" and "she" are pronounced simply as [i], or at times the speaker may use both interchangeably. This feature of Liberian English parallels the lack of gender specific pronouns in the native Niger-Congo languages native. On the following page is a pronoun chart reflecting the modified pronunciation of Liberian Vernacular English.

| Pronoun Chart of Liberian Vernacular English | | Singular | | | Plural | | |
|---|---|---|---|---|---|---|---|
| | | Subject | Object | Reflexive | Subject | Object | Reflexive |
| 1st person | | A [a] | me [mi] | mysef [masɛf] | we [wi] | us [ʌs] | awasef [awasɛf] |
| 2nd person | | yu [ju] | yu [ju] | yosef [josɛf] | yor [jɔ] | yor [jɔ] | yorsef [jɔsɛf] |
| 3rd person | Masculine | he [hi] | heen [hi] | heensef [hisɛf] | dey [de] | e | demsef [demsɛf] |
| 3rd person | Feminine | she [ʃi] | hur [hɔ] | hursef [hɔsɛf] | | | |
| 3rd person | Neuter | ih [ɪ] | ih [ɪ] | ihsef [ɪsɛf] | | | |

## Possession:

Whereas Standard English usually designates possession with the suffix (–'s), Liberian English indicates the same simply by word order. The object of belonging follows immediately after the possessor. For instance,

*George woman name Decontee.*
"George's wife is named Decontee."

The auxiliary *geh* "get" is also used to designate possession. It takes the place of the "has," "had" and "have" of Standard English. For example,

*A de one wa get it.*
I the one what get it.
"I am the one who has it."

The use of possessive pronouns (his, her, etc.) in Liberian English is less common than in Standard English. Instead, the language makes frequent use of the pronoun *fo* "for" in this regard. So, rather than saying "That's his book," one would say *De book fo heen.* "The book for him."

## Emphasis:

There are several ways in which emphasis can be given in Liberian Vernacular English.

[O] is often used at the end of their sentences as a sort of verbal exclamation mark, as is common in many of the native Niger-Congo languages. For example,

*Da na me o!*
That not me o!
"It wasn't me!"

Emphasis can also be given through the doubling of words. This is most often heard with adjectives and adverbs and is another common feature of the native languages. For example,

*He ain know ih too good good.*
He ain't know it too good good.
"He doesn't know it very well."

Similar to the Standard English "even", the word *sef* "self" is also used at the end of clauses for emphatic purposes. For example,

*Dog sef cyan eat da foo.*
Dog self can't eat that food.
"Even a dog couldn't eat that food."

"All" can be used in a similar fashion as in,

*Baboon all wan to become presiden.*
Baboon all want to become president.
"Even the chimpanzee wants to become the president."

To emphasize a whole sentence, *sef* can also be used.

*Da woman cyan cook potato greens sef!*
That woman can't cook potato greens self!
"That woman can't even cook potato greens!"

## Grammar Sketch: Verb Phrases

The usage of verbs in Liberian Vernacular English differs significantly from Standard English. Whereas verbs in Standard English are marked primarily for tense (in reference to an action's place in time), in Liberian English has a heavy emphasis on aspect and mood (referencing the frequency or state of completion of an action).

# Past Action:

Liberian English speakers often do not mark the simple past tense. This is especially true for verbs with an irregular past tense forms such as "find" and "found." For example,

*He fine ouh hih ma sick.*

He find out his ma sick.

"He found out that his mother is sick."

Speakers of Liberian English will commonly use a past progressive form in place of the simple past. This is doing through the use of the auxiliary *wa* "was" and the –ing suffix on the verb.

*He wa needing to go to de doctor.*

He was needing to go to the doctor.

"He needed to go to the doctor."

To indicate that an action has been completed, the marker *fini* "finish" is used.

*He fini go een town.*

He finish go in town.

"He has gone to town."

*Na* "now" also functions in the same way as *fini* but is slightly less common.

*Papa na come.*

Papa now come.

"Papa has come."

Both *fini* and *na* are equivalent to the Standard English "has." This word may also be used in Liberian Vernacular English, although the rules of pronunciation mean that "has" along with other forms such as "have" and "had" are all pronounced as *ha*.

*De mayor ha come to campaign fo reelection.*

"The mayor had come to campaign for reelection".

## Unrealized Action:

Linguists use the term "irrealis" to refer to events that have not yet been realized. These may be future events, or events that are conditional on certain circumstances. Liberian English has several ways or marking irrealis.

For future actions Liberian English uses *will* [wɪ] just as in Standard English.

*He will go een town.*

"He will go in town."

Some basilectical speakers may also use *go* as a future tense marker.

*A go buy cassava fron de markeh.*

I go buy cassava from the market.

"I will buy cassava from the market."

*Will* may also be used in place of "would" to indicate conditional events.

*If A go to America A will be too happy.*

If I go to America I will be too happy.

"If I could go to America I would be very happy."

The incompletive aspect marker *coming* [kãmĩ] is frequently used in reference to future events. This usually signifies that an action is just about to take place.

*He coming go een town.*

He coming go in town.

"He is about to go to town."

To indicate past conditional events *wa coming* and *wa going* are used.

> *If dey wa coming elect da man he wa going bring noda mo war.*
>
> If they was coming elect that man he was going to bring another more war.
>
> "If they would have elected that man he would have brought another war."

## Progressive Action:

Like Standard English, Liberian English indicates progressive action simply use the -ing form of the verb.

> *He going een town.*
>
> He going in town.
>
> "He is going to town."

The past progressive is marked by the same form plus the auxiliary *wa* "was."

> *A wa going to de markeh de tam A see Sumo.*
>
> I was going to the market the time I see Sumo.
>
> "I was going to the market when I saw Sumo."

Past progressive action which continues to the present is marked with *been.*

> *Susan been fising kuway ewasince.*
>
> Susan been fixing kool-aid ever since.
>
> "Susan has been making sweet drinks for a long time."

## Habitual Action:

The most common way of marking repeating or habitual action is with the marker *can.*

*Princess can lie.*

"Princess is a liar."

*My fren can be to de video club hoday.*

My friend can be to the video club whole day.

"My friend is always at the video club."

## Hortative Action:

This term refers to words that urge or strongly encourage a specific course of action. By far the most common way to do this in Liberian English is through the use of the modal verb *muh* "must."

*Yu muh gii me five dala.*

You must give me five dollar.

"Give me five dollars."

Liberian English also makes use of *shu* "should" in this regard.

*A shu go to school today?*

I should go to school today?

"Should I go to school today?"

S*uppose to* is another common hortative marker in Liberian Vernacular English, used rather than "ought to."

*Willie suppose to be feeding de rabbit, buh he go play wif hih*
    *fren dem.*

Willie supposed to be feeding the rabbit, but he go play with his
    friend them.

"Willie is supposed to be feeding the rabbits, but he went to play
    with his friends."

## Copula:

Another notable feature of Liberian Vernacular English grammar is the "missing" verbs of being: i.e. *is, are* and *am*. Linguists refer to these words as the copula. The missing copula is common in English-based creoles around the world. In Liberia the use of the copula is more common among people who have undergone formal education, but even literate speakers may use it inconsistently. Below is a brief description of how various types of clauses are formed in Liberian English without the copula.

In Standard English, the copula is used in attributive clauses that link a noun with an adjective. In Liberian Vernacular English, no copula is necessary.

*Da man tall.*
"That man is tall."

In locative clauses, which describe the location of an object, the copula is also omitted.

*De boy yeh.*
"The boy is here."

The word *da* "that" can function as the copula in equative clauses, in which one thing is compared with another.

*Edward da big man.*
"Edward is a big man (important person)."

*Yu tink breh da goo foo?*
"You think bread is a good food?"

## Comparison:

The most common way to compare one thing with another is through the use of the word *pas* "past."

*She fine pas do ola women dem.*

She fine past those other women them.

"She is more beautiful than those other women."

Another way comparisons can be made is by using *den* or "then."

*He big den hih cousin.*

He big then his cousin.

"He is bigger than his cousin."

## Negation:

All of the languages native to Liberia are tonal and changes of pitch are used to indicate lexical and grammatical meaning. One of the most fascinating aspects of Liberian Vernacular English is the presence of grammatical tone. This can most clearly be seen in the use of high tone for negative auxiliaries.

In Liberian English, the negative auxiliary *na* "not" is distinguished from the completive aspect marker *na* "now" only by its high tone. This can be seen with the contrasting sentences below.

| | |
|---|---|
| *Papa na come.* | *Papa ná come.* |
| Papa now come. | Papa not come. |
| "Papa has come." | "Papa has not come." |

Another contrasting minimal pair are the words for "can" and "can't". Both are pronounced [kæ] with the negative being indicated by the high tone. For the purpose of a practical orthography, in this book "can't" is spelled *cyan*.

| | |
|---|---|
| *He can mek ih.* | *He cyan mek it* |
| He can make it. | He can not make it. |

Another common way to negate clauses is by use of the word *ain* [ẽ] (from Southern U.S. "ain't"*).*

*A ain coming staylong deh.*

I ain't coming stay long there.

"I won't be there long."

Double negatives, while considered incorrect in Standard English, are widely used in Liberian English. For example:

*He ain newa com yah.*

He ain't never come here.

"He never came here."

In Liberian English statements of description are often stated in a negative form. For example:

*Ih na easy to brush farm.*

It not easy to brush farm.

"It's difficult to clear a farm."

*Fron yah deh na far.*

From here there not far.

"It's not far from here to there."

# Dictionary

This dictionary is an attempt to catalog some of Liberian Vernacular English's unique nuances and to define unfamiliar words borrowed from other languages. This is not a comprehensive lexicon of Liberian English. The majority of the words in the language are derived from American or British English. Therefore, except in cases where the Liberian Vernacular English pronunciation varies significantly from Standard English varieties, only English words with unique meanings are included. Many examples of borrowed words are listed and their origin is stated when known. Examples of the use of these words are intended to give readers a better understanding of cultural context in which they exists. A word for word translation of the example sentences is included as well as an idiomatic translation in American English.

## Abbreviations:

*conj.* Conjunction

*adj* Adjective

*adv* Adverb

*pro* Pronoun

*n* Noun

*v* Verb

# A

**ABC** [e bi si] *n.*, Used in place of "alphabet." *Pekin, yu know yo ABC?* (Pekin, you know your ABC?) "Little boy, do you know your alphabet?"

**arm robba:** [ã:m ɹabɔ] "armed robber" *n.*, A thief who uses weapons such as machetes or guns to commit robbery. The most common term for a thief in Liberia is **rogue**, although this term is usually reserved for those who commit petty theft. *Las night to Gbarnga dey say arm robba enta one woman hus an steal plenty money fron hur.* (Last night to Gbarnga they say armed robber enter one woman house and steal plenty money from her.) "They say that last night in Gbarnga armed robbers broke into a woman's house and stole a lot of money from her."

**abo:** [ebo] "able" *v.*, 1. To be capable of doing something. *He pa, he ain abo ih.* (His part, he ain't able it.) "As for him, he can't do it." 2. To overcome, defeat, take on something. *Yu abo me?* (You able me?) "Can you take me on?"

**abuse:** [abius] *v.*, To curse, belittle, insult, etc. Does not connote as serious a grievance as in Standard English. *De teacha abuse me de tam A mek mistek.* (The teacher abuse me the time I make mistake.) "The teacher ridiculed me when I made a mistake." See also **cauz** and **swear**.

**accra ground pea:** [akɹa grʌ pi] *n.*, A small white nut commonly sold in the market. Chewed like kola, and then spit out.

**AFL:** [e ɛf ɛl] *n.*, The Armed Forces of Liberia. The official army of Liberia.

**African show:** [afɹikã ʃo] *n.*, Used in reference to the popular Nigerian soap operas. *Ain yu see da African show to Momo play las ni?* (Ain't you see that African show to Momo place last night?) "Didn't you see the soap opera at Momo's house last night?"

**African signs:** [afɹikã saĩs] "African science" *n.*, Witchcraft, sorcery. Liberians generally have a strong belief in occult forces. This term positively compares the traditional African occultic sources of power with the power of Western science. *De zoe dem owna African signs strong pa de kwi medicine.* (The zoe them own of African science strong past the kwi medicine.) "The zo's witchcraft is stronger than Western medicine."

**agen:** [edʒɛ̃] "agent" *n.*, A spy. *De tam de rebo dem kesh da man, dey accuse heen say he agen fo Charles Taylor.* (The time the rebel them catch that man they accuse him say he agent for Charles Taylor.) "When the rebels caught that man, they accused him of being a spy for Charles Taylor."

**agin**: [əgĩ] "again" *adv.*, 1. At this time. *A ain wan some agin.* (I ain't want some again.) "I don't want any at this time." 2. Anymore. *Wa happing da man cyan come yeh agin?* (What happen that man can't come here again?) "Why doesn't that man come here anymore?"

**agree**: [əgɹi] *v.*, To consent, concur. *A wan carry yo car eentown, yu agree?* (I want carry your car in town, you agree?) "I want to take your car in town. Is that alright?"

**agro oil**: [ægɹo ɔj] *n.*, Vegetable oil. Used primarily for frying. Otherwise palm oil is preferred. *De kwi man say he wan so yu muh fis hih soup wif agro oil.* (The kwi man say he want so you must fix his soup with agro oil.) "The white man said you should make his sauce with vegetable oil."

**aih coo**: [ɛ ku] "air cool" *n.*, Air-conditioning. *De play too heateh. Yu muh plea puh on de aih coo.* (The place too heated. You must please put on the air cool.) "It's too hot here. Please turn on the air conditioning."

**ain**: [ẽ] "ain't" *adv.*, A general negating word. *A ain yo small boy.* (I ain't your small boy.) "I'm not your inferior." See also **na** and **don**.

**all**: [ɔ] *adj.*, And all, everyone. *Baboon all wan to become presiden.* (Baboon all want to become President.) "Everyone, including the chimpanzee, wants to become president."

**alligata**: [alɪgetɔ] "alligator" *n.*, A crocodile. Liberia does not have any true alligators, but is home to the Nile crocodile (*Crocodylus niloticus*), and two dwarf crocodile species: *Osteolaemus tetraspis* and *Crocodylus cataphractus*. All are commonly referred to as *alligata*. A potent traditional poison is made in Liberia from crocodile bile. *De chief say de tam yu kesh alligata yu muh bring ih to heen.* (The chief say the time you catch alligator you must bring it to him.) "The chief said when you catch a crocodile, you should bring it to him."

**alligata peppa**: [alɪgetɔ pɛpa] "alligator pepper" *n.*, A type of spice. See **mala**.

**Alligata Society**: [alɪgetɔ sosaɹti] "alligator society" *n.*, A secret organization whose members are believed to be able to transform into crocodiles through occultic power. See also **Lepor Society**.

**all two**: [ɔ tu] *adj.*, Both. *Yu wan so A muh clean all two fish?* (You want so I must clean all two fish?) "Do you want me to clean both of the fish?"

**Americo-Liberian**: [ameɹiko laɪbiɹẽ] *n.*, Descendents of the freed slaves who founded the Republic of Liberia.

**ans bear**: [æs bɛ:] "ants bear" *n.*, The pangolin. *Manis spp.* An ant-eating mammal covered in reptile-like scales. *Ma unco kill one ans bear een de bush yestuday.* (My uncle killed one ants bear in the bush yesterday.) "My uncle killed a pangolin in the forest yesterday."

**attend**: [atɛ̃] *v.*, To go to school. This verb does not require a specific object in Liberian English. *Een Greenville A wa attending, buh yeh pa dey ain geh no goo school.* (In Greenville I was attending, but here part they ain't get no good school.) "I was going to school in Greenville, but as for here, there are no good schools."

**ATU**: [e ti ju] *n.*, Anti-Terrorism Unit. An elite squad of fighters loyal to Charles Taylor who during the civil war were infamous for their brutality.

**aunty**: [æti] *n.*, Aunt. This, like other Liberian kinship terms, is often used in a much broader sense than in Standard English. *Aunty* can be applied to older female relatives or as a term of respect in addressing strangers. *Aunty Korpu na come fron Kollie Town.* (Auntie Korpu now come from Kollie Town.) "Mrs. Korpu just came from Kollie Town."

**ay-yah**: [e:ja] *interj.*, An interjection of frustration. *Ay-yah! Wa happen yo fini ditey yosef?* (Ay-yah! What happen you finish dirty yourself.) "Good grief! Why did you go get yourself all dirty?"

# B

**ba**: [ba] *n.*, A friend. From the Bassa language $\overline{gba}$ "friend." *Eh ba, plea gii me chance.* (Eh ba, please give me chance.) "Come on, buddy, please give me a break."

**baboon**: [bæbū:] *n.*, The chimpanzee. *Pan troglodytes.* Sometimes pronounced "bamboo." *No monkey work baboon draw yeh!* (No monkey work baboon draw here!) "Nobody is going to take the credit for another's hard work here."

**babi**: [babi] *n.*, Foosball. A table-top soccer game. *Dey wa having plenty babi yeh befo, buh de police stop ih beca do grenna boy dem wa meking plenty plenty palava fo da ting bisneh.* (They was having plenty babi here before, but the police stop it because those grenna boy them was making plenty plenty palaver for the thing business.) "There used to be a lot of foosball tables here, but the police put a stop to it because those trouble-making boys were fighting a lot over them."

**baby ma**: [bebi ma] *n.*, 1. The mother of a young child. *Wa play yu going, baby ma?* (What place you going, baby ma?) "Where are you going, baby's mother?" 2. A woman who bore a man's child, but is not legally married to him. *My baby ma to de hus.* (My baby ma to the house.) "My baby's mother is at the house."

**back**: [bæk˙] *v.*, To put on one's back. *Mamee, yu cyan back de baby so we can go? (Mamee, you can't back the baby so we can go?)* "Mamee, can't you put the baby on your back so we can go?"

**baf fence**: [bæf fɛs] *n.*, An outdoors enclosed area used for bathing. Usually made with raffia palm or bamboo. *De hot wata eenside de baf fence.* (The hot water inside the baf fence.) "The hot water is inside the bath fence."

**balance**: [bælǣs] *adj.*, The remainder, left over. *De balance rice leave een de cookpot.* (The balance rice leave in the cookpot.) "The leftover rice is in the pot."

**bamboo**: [bābu] *n.*, Used in Liberia to refer to the raffia palm (*Raffia spp.*) rather than true bamboo (*Bambusa spp.*), which are called **reed**. The hard, long stems of the raffia palm are used to build a variety of items and the leaves are used for thatch. *A coming fis bamboo mat to puh owa my room.* (I coming fix bamboo mat to put over my room.) "I'm getting ready to weave a raffia mat to use as a ceiling in my room." See **papoo**.

**bamboo bed**: [bābu bɛ] *n.*, A simple homemade bed made from raffia stems. Common in rural areas.

35

**bamboo wine:** [bãbu waĩ] *n.,* See **palm wine.**

**bamboo wolum:** [bãbu wolũ] "bamboo worm" *n.,* Large beetle grubs that can be found living in raffia palms. Considered by many to be a delicacy, raw or roasted. *A coming roas some bamboo wolum. Yu wan som?* (I coming roast some bamboo worm. You want some?) "I am going to roast some grubs. Do you want any?"

**Bandi:** [bãdi] *n.,* An ethnic group native to the Kolahun district of Lofa County. Population is approximately 100,000. They speak a language in the Southwest-Mande language family, closely related to Mende. *Ma ole ma da Bandi, buh A cyan speak de tribe.* (My old ma that Bandi, but I can't speak the tribe.) "My mother is a Bandi, but I can't speak the language."

**Bandi quick service:** [badi kwɪ sɛɹvɪ] *n.,* A simple, red-oil based sauce cooked quickly to serve unexpected guests. Similar to another popular Vai dish called **tu jai kpono.**

**banyo:** [baɲo] 1. *v.,* To sell at a greatly reduced price. From Sierra Leonian Krio. *De way my greens plenty, A coming banyo ih.* (The way my greens plenty, I coming banyo it.) "Because I have a lot of greens, I am going to sell them cheaply." 2. *adj.,* Cheap, inexpensive. *A buy da banyo lappa.* (I buy that banyo lappa.) "I bought that cheap lappa."

**barb:** [ba:b] *v.,* To cut hair. *Eh ba, yu muh fine nyew razor ble befo yu barb me!* (Eh ba, you must find new razor blade before you barb me!) "Hey buddy, you should get a new razor blade before cutting my hair!"

**barbing saloon:** [ba:bĩ salũ:] *n.,* A haircutting booth. *Ifan A cu jus geh lil money, A will open one barbing saloon.* (If I could just get little money, I will open one barbing saloon.) "If I could just get a little money, I would open a haircutting booth."

**barbing shears:** [ba:bĩ ʃɪɹs] *n.,* Electric clippers.

**Bassa:** [basa] *n.,* A large ethnic group of about 400,000 people. They speak a language in the Kwa family. Primarily found in Grand Bassa County, they were also traditionally located in Mesurado and were one of the first groups encountered by the settlers. *Dey say de Bassa ole peepo dem sell deh lan fo boney.* (They say the Bassa old people them sell their land for boney.) "They say the Bassa's ancestors sold their land (to the Americo-Liberians) for dried fish."

**ba way:** [bæ wej] "Bad way" *adv.,* Very much so, greatly, a lot. *Solo an Jalla resembo ba way.* (Solo and Jalla resemble bad way.) "Solo and Jalla look a lot alike."

**beard-beard**: [biabia] *adj.*, Used to describe someone with prominent facial hair. *Ain yu see da beard-beard man passing so?* (Ain't you see that beard beard man passing so?) "Don't you see that guy with the big beard walking over there?"

**beat**: [bi] 1. *v.*, To spank. Does not necessary imply abuse as in Standard English. *Stop causing noise befo A beat yu!* (Stop causing noise before I beat you!) "If you don't be quiet, I'm going to spank you!" See also **flok** and **soak**. 2. *v.*, To play a percussive musical instrument. *Da woman can beat the sasa fine!* (That woman can beat the sasa fine.) "That lady plays the goard rattle well!" 3. *v.*, To hull rice in a mortar. *She muh beat de rice befo we cook ih.* (She must beat the rice before we cook it.) "She has to hull the rice before we cook it." 4. *v.*, An engine's running. *A cyan sleep wif da engine beating so.* (I can't sleep with that engine beating so.) "I can't sleep with that engine running like that."

**beat time**: [bi tãm] *v.*, To defeat an opponent. *James can beat all of yor tam een eating bisneh.* (James can beat all of y'all's time in eating business) "James can beat all of you when it comes to eating lots of food."

**beep**: [bip] *v.*, To call a cell phone briefly for the purpose of notifying the other person that you have low credit and want him to call you back. Also called **flash**. *Ma man, wa happing hoday yo jus beeping me?* (My man, what happen whole day you just beeping me.) "Buddy, why are you always beeping me?"

**beg**: [beg] *v.*, 1. To ask, to plead. Not considered as strong as it is in Standard English and it can be used for just about any request. A strong plea will often be accompanied with the phrase *A hole yo foot.* (I hold your foot.) *A beg yu, man. Yu muh plea gii me small co wata.* (I beg you, man. You must please give me small cold water.) "Please man, give me a little loose change." 2. This word can also be used in the sense of "Give me a break!" *Yu wan so A muh credih yu two hundreh dala? A beg yu! A ain reesh man.* (You want so I must credit you two hundred dollars? I beg you! I ain't rich man.) "You want me to lend you two hundred dollars? Give me a break! I'm not a rich man."

**ben**: [bẽ] "bend" *v.*, To turn, bear. *De tam yu reesh on de main ro, yu muh ben right skrate.* (The time you reach on the main road, you must bend right straight.) "When you get to the main road, you should turn right immediately."

**ben-ben**: [bẽbẽ] "bend-bend" *adj.*, Crooked, twisted. *Wa happing yu bring so so ben-ben plank?* (What happen you bring so so bend bend plank?) "Why did you bring only crooked boards?"

**ben de elbow**: [bɛ̃ dɛ ɛlbo] "bend the elbow" *v.*, To get drunk. *A see David to de niclub benning de elbow.* (I see David to the nightclub bending the elbow.) "I saw David at the club getting drunk."

**bennyseed**: [bɛnisi] *n.*, Sesame seeds. *Semamun indicum. Benniseed can be too swee wen yu mek ih wif breh.* (Benniseed can be too sweet when you make it with bread.) "Sesame seeds are delicious when cooked with bread."

**behine**: [bihãĩ] "behind" *prep.*, 1. To nag, insist. *Wa happing hoday A muh be behine yu to do dis lil piece oh job?* (What happen whole day I must be behind you to do this little piece of job.) "Why do I have to be after you constantly to make you do this little thing?" 2. To pursue, to follow. *A ain know wa mek ih he alway running behine woman bisneh.* (I ain't know what make it he always running behind woman business.) "I don't know why he's always chasing after women." 3. To be possessed by a spirit or supernatural power. *Johnny geh some kin oh jina behine heen wa can mek heen fall off.* (Johnny get some kind of jina behind him what can make him fall off.) Johnny is haunted by some kind of spirit that makes him go crazy.

**Belle**: [bɛlɛ] *n.*, A small Kwa-speaking people group of about 13,000 people found in northern Gbarpolu County. Surrounded by the **Bandi, Lorma, Kpelle** and **Gola**, they are isolated culturally and linguistically. They often refer to themselves as the *Kuuwa. De Belle can speak all de tribe.* (The Belle can speak all the tribe.) "The Belle speak all the different languages."

**belly**: [bɛli] 1. *n.*, The stomach, abdomen. *Betta belly bus den goo foo wase.* (Better belly bust than good food waste.) "It's better for your stomach to burst than for good food to go to waste." See also **guh**. 2. *n.*, The state of being pregnant. *Korpu geh tdee mon belly.* (Korpu get three month belly.) "Korpu is three months pregnant." 3. *v.*, To *give belly* is to impregnate. *Da he de one gii Decontee belly.* (That he the one give Decontee belly.) "He's the one who got Decontee pregnant." 4. *v.*, To *move de belly* or *spoil de belly* is to have an abortion. *Mary say she ain wan no baby, so da haccome she spoil de belly.* (Mary say she ain't want no baby, so that how come she spoil the belly.) "Mary said she didn't want a baby, so that's why she had an abortion."

**besse**: [bɛsɛ] *n.*, A gossip. A shortened form of "busybody." Borrowed from Sierra Leonean Krio. See also **chechepolay** and **gehdah**.

**big**: [bi] "big" *adj.*, Used instead of large, huge, immense, vast, etc. Often doubled for emphasis. *Deh one big big cotton tree to de village.* (There one big big cotton tree to the village.) "There's a huge silk cotton tree near the village."

**biga boy**: [bika bɔɪ] "bigger boy" *n.*, A big shot, well-to-do man. Slang. *Since Stephen become biga boy he cyan ride bus agin.* (Since Stephen become bigger boy he can't ride bus again.) "Since Steven became a big shot he doesn't ride the bus anymore."

**big heart**: [bi haː] "big heart" *n.*, Prideful, boastful, arrogant. *De way Beyan can tok show he geh big heart.* (The way Beyan can talk show he got big heart.) "The way Beyan talks shows he is a arrogant person." See also **biggity**.

**biggity**: [bɪgɪti] *n.*, Pride, arrogance. *Jacob looking too biggity since he star woking fo de gowamen.* (Jacob looking too biggity since he start working for the government.) "Jacob has been acting arrogant since he started working for the government."

**big man**: [bi mɛ̃] "big man" *n.*, Someone in a position of authority, usually with the government. *Some oh doh big man dem fron Monrovia coming be to de program.* (Some of those big man them from Monrovia coming be to the program.) "Some of those important people from Monrovia are going to be at the program."

**big shot**: [bi ʃa] "big shot" *n.*, An important person. Not used sarcastically as in American English. *De man da real big shot da.* (The man that real big shot that.) "That man is a very important person."

**bill**: [bɪl] *n.*, Fishing bait. *A wan go to de swam to dig some bill.* (I want go to the swamp to dig some bill.) "I want to go to the swamp to dig some bait."

**billhook**: [bɪl hʊkˈ] *n.*, A small cutting tool with a curved blade. Commonly used in rice cultivation. *He say he muh sharp de billhook befo he go on de farm.* (He say he must sharp the billhook before he go on the farm.) "He said he has to sharpen the billhook before he goes to the farm."

**bisneh**: [bɪsnɪ] "business" *n.*, 1. Manner of doing things. *A ain love too mush oh halahala bisneh.* (I ain't love too much of holler holler business.) "I don't like a lot of confusion and shouting. "2. An issue, matter pertaining to. *Da dis ting bisneh wa mek ih so A keshing hard tam.)* "That this thing business what make it so I catching hard time.) "It's this matter that's causing trouble for me." 3. Sexual experience. *Da lil geh ain know man bisneh yeh.* (That little girl ain't know man business yet.) "That young girl is a virgin." 4. This word can also be used after a subordinating conjunction to mean "because." *De tam yu see me coming bisneh yu muh na jus tink say A behine yu fo money.* (The time you see me coming business you must not just think say I behind you for money.) "When you see me coming you shouldn't just think that I am after you for money." 5. A business enterprise. *She ain been making plenty money wif her lil gobuychop bisneh.* (She ain't been making plenty money with her little gobuychop business.) "She hasn't been making much money with her resale business." 6. This word is often heard in Liberia in reference to someone liking someone else. One is not said to just like someone, they rather like their "business." *Deh one woman to New Kru Town wa luf my bisneh too mush.* (There one woman to New Kru Town what love my business too much.) "There's a woman in New Kru Town who likes me a lot."

**biri**: [biɾi] *n.,* A circumcision rite for young boys practiced by Muslim majority ethnic groups such as the Vai and Mandingo. Considered to be a godly substitute for the traditional Poro initiations.

**biskih**: [bɪskɪ] "biscuit" *n.,* Used instead of "cookie." *Go buy five dala biskih.* (Go buy five dollar biscuit.) "Go buy a five dollar pack of cookies."

**bitaball**: [bɪtabɔ] "bitterball" *n.,* A small bitter tasting vegetable similar to an eggplant. *Solanum aethiopicum.* A popular ingredient for sauces. *De bitterball dey selling to de markeh too small small.* (The bitterball they selling to de market too small small.) "The bitterballs they are selling at the market are very small."

**bite and blow**: [baɪt ã blo] *idiom.,* To take advantage of someone without them noticing. Comes from an old wives tale about rats, which are known to occasionally eat small pieces of flesh off sleeping people. The rats are said to blow on the skin softly to numb the pain. *De way Peter play krokroji on de bossman, he rally bite an blow!* (The way Peter play krokroji on the bossman, he really bite and blow.) "Peter really pulled one over on the boss!"

**black**: [blæk˺] *adj.,* Dark skinned. Considered unattractive to most Liberians. *Jenkins da short black man wa can be to de shop deh.* (Jenkins that short black man what can be to the shop there.) "Jenkins is that short, dark fellow who is usually at the store." Contrasted with **bright**.

**blackback**: [blæ bak˺] *n.,* A dark colored duiker (antelope.) *Cephalophus niger* or *Cephalophus ogilbyi. De hunta kill tdee blackback de tam he wa ontop de mountain.* (The hunter kill three blackback the time he was on top the mountain.) "The hunter killed three blackbacks when he was on the mountain."

**black bagga**: [blæk˺ bægɔ] "black bagger" *n.,* A traveling salesman who sells questionable medicine out of a black briefcase. Often considered to be quacks. *A wa coming go to de clinic wen A buddah wif one black bagger.* (I was coming go to the clinic when I butt up with one black bagger.) "I was getting ready to go to the clinic when I met a traveling medicine salesman."

**black monkey**: [blæk˺ mɔ̃kɛ] *n.*, 1. Colobus Monkey. *Colobus polykomos polykomos*. A black monkey with a white tail. *De black monkey dem been spoiling my rice farm.* (The black monkey them been spoiling my rice farm.) "The colobus monkeys have been ruining my rice farm." 2. A term of insult. Monkeys are considered by Liberians to be extremely ugly.

**black stone**: [blæk˺ stõ] *n.*, A small piece of cow bone charred to become extremely dry and porous. Placed over snakebites to draw out the poison. *Ih goo to have black stone to de village so anytam snek boin somone, ih won kill dem.* (It good to have black stone to the village so any time snake bite someone, it won't kill them.) "It's good to keep black stones in the village, so a snake bite won't be deadly."

**blade**: [bled] *n.*, Stylish clothes. Slang. *Moses puh on hih blade to go walkabout.* (Moses put on his blade to go walkabout.) "Moses put on his Sunday best to go stroll around town." See also **zoot** and **shako**.

**block**: [blak˺] *v.*, To obstruct, to be in the way. *Two car mek accident. Na dey blocking da ro.* (Two car make accident. Now they're blocking that road.) "Two cars had an accident and are blocking that road.)

**blood tableh**: [blə tablɛ] "blood tablet" *n.*, Used instead of "vitamin pill." *De docta say a muh tek dee blood tableh dem.* (The doctor say I must take these blood tablet them.) "The doctor said I should take these vitamins."

**blood fish**: [blə fiʃ] *n.*, Atlantic Bluefin Tuna. *Thunnus thynnus.*

**blow**: [blo] *v.*, To hit, punch. *De tam da frisky pekin cauz Ole Man Flomo, de papay wa coming blow heen.* (The time that frisky pekin curse Old Man Flomo, the papay was coming blow him.) "When that rude little boy insulted Mr. Flomo, the old man was about to punch him."

**bluff**: [bləf] *v.*, To show off, to flaunt. Does not imply deception as in the Standard English usage. *Sam na need eyeglasses. He can jus be wearing ih to bluff.* (Sam not need eyeglasses. He can just be wearing it to bluff.) "Sam doesn't need glasses. He just wears them to show off."

**bluffajoe**: [blʌfad͡ʒo] *n.*, A person who likes to "bluff" or show off. *Samuel zooting wif hih shades an hih coat-suit. He real bluffajoe.* (Samuel zooting with his shades and his coat-suit. He real bluffajoe.) "Samuel is all dressed up with his sunglasses and a suit. He is a real showoff."

**bluffing clo**: [blʌfi klo] "bluffing clothes" *n.*, Fancy clothes worn to impress. *Hoday Mary can jus be passing een de street wif hur bluffing clo.* (Whole day Mary can just be passing in the street with her bluffing clothes.) "Mary is always promenading on the street in her fancy clothes."

**boa-constructa**: [bokɔstɹətə] "boa-constrictor" *n.*, Python. True boas do not live in Liberia. There are two species native to Liberia; the large rock python, *Python sabea*, which can reach lengths of over 20 ft and is quite dangerous, and the smaller ball python, *Python regius*. *Las yeah A wa untop de mountain wen A see one big boa-constructa swallowing raccoon.* (Last year I was on top the mountain when I see one big boa-constrictor swallowing raccoon.) " Last year I was on top of the mountain when I saw a big python swallowing a civet."

**boc-boc**: [bɔbɔ] *interj.*, Said when standing outside a door in lieu of knocking.

**body bra**: [badi bɹa] *n.*, A one-piece women's bathing suit. Liberia women generally do not engage in recreational swimming but may wear these under their clothes for support.

**boku**: [boku] *adj.*, Many, abundant. From the French language. *Deh boku fish een da wata.* (There boku fish in that water.) "There are lots of fish in that river." See also **plenty**.

**bone docta**: [bõ dakta] "bone doctor" *n.*, A traditional bone-setter. Many of these practitioners are quite skilled in setting broken bones through careful realignment of fractures. Some also employ sympathetic magic. They will commonly break the leg of a chicken and tell the patient that when the chicken's leg is healed, their leg will also be healed.

**boney**: [boni] *n.*, Smoked or dried fish, commonly herring. *Boney too dear dee few days.* (Boney too dear these few days.) "Dried fish is really expensive now."

**boogooman**: [bukumẽ] *n.*, The boogie-man. Greatly feared by young children in Liberia . *Da lil geh say she ain wan so de boogooman muh kesh hur.* (That little girl say she ain't want so the boogyman must catch her.) "That little girl said she doesn't want the boogie-man to catch her." See also **heart man**.

**book**: [bʊkˀ] *n.*, Used metaphorically in reference to Western-style education. In Liberia, to "know book" is to be educated. *Wen dis man star to know book, he coming be one big gowamen man.* (When this man start to know book, he will be a big government man.) "When this man is educated, he will be a powerful government official."

**book peepo**: [bʊ pipo] "book people" *n.*, The educated class. People who *"know book." De book peepo dem ain geh tam fo we de farma dem.* (The book people them ain't get time for we the farmer them.) "The educated class doesn't care about us farmers."

**bobo**: [bobo] *n.*, A deaf/mute person. Probably borrowed from the Mandingo or Kpelle language. *De tam A wen to de papay house, A meh one bobo boy to de yar deh.* (The time I went to the papay house, I met one bobo boy to the yard there.) "When I went to the old man's house, I met a mute boy in the yard."

**body**: [badi] *n.*, A muscular physique. Slang. *Da man geh body.* (That man get body.) "That man is well built."

**body man**: [badi mẽ] *n.*, A muscular, well-built man. *Saki go to AFL training. Na he real body man.* (Saki go to AFL training. Now he real body man.) "Saki went to the Armed Forces of Liberia training. Now he is a real muscleman."

**boid**: [bɔɪ] *n.*, A bird. *Ih doh small small boid dem wa can be spoiling my farm.* (It those small small bird them what can be spoiling my farm.) "It's those little birds that ruin my farm."

**boin**: [bɔĩ] "burn" *v.*, To bite. *Tek tam befo da dog boin yu!* (Take time before that dog burn you.) "Be careful so that dog doesn't bite you."

**boin farm**: [bɔĩ 'fã:m] "burn farm" *v.*, Liberians typically practice what is known as "slash-and-burn" agriculture. A patch of forest is first cleared by hand. After the foliage has had time to dry, fire is set to it. The fire destroys weeds and the ashes fertilize the soil in preparation for the rice to be planted there. *A wan boin farm, buh de rain giving me hard tam.* (I want burn farm, but the rain giving me hard time.) "I want to burn my farm, but the rain is making things difficult for me."

**boin palm oil**: [bɔĩ pã ɔj] "burnt palm oil" *n.*, Clarified red palm oil. Has a longer shelf life than unrefined palm oil, but is considered less tasty.

**bore**: [bɔ] v., To pierce or drill through an object. *De baby ma fini bore de baby yeh fo yehring* (The baby ma finish bore the baby ear for earring.) "The baby's mother pierced the baby's ear to put in an earring."

**born**: [bɔ̃] 1. *v.*, To give birth. *He an hih woman born one fine pekin.* (He and his woman born one fine pekin.) "He and his wife gave birth to a beautiful little boy." 2. *adj.*, One's biological family. Used to distinguish one's biological parents or children from other relatives who may be called the same out of respect. *She my born ma.* (She my born ma.) "She's my real mother."

**born town**: [bɔ̃ tã] *n.*, One's birthplace. *Zorzor my born town.* (Zorzor my born town.) "Zorzor is my birthplace."

**borrow**: [baɹo] *v.*, To lend or loan. *Yu muh plea borrow me yo cycle, yah?* (You must please borrow me your cycle, you hear?) "Could you please lend me your bike?"

**bossman**: [bausmẽ] *n.*, A term of respect for an authority figure. *Ma boss-man sen me een town to buy fuel.* (My bossman sent me in town to buy fuel.) "My boss sent me in town to buy diesel fuel." This term is often used to designate respect in the context of a patron/client relationship. In Liberia those in a position of power and wealth (patrons) are expected to provide for the educational, financial, material, etc., needs of those under them (clients.) The clients are in turn expected to be loyal to their patrons and reciprocate the aid they receive with acts of service or token gifts such as fruit, vegetables or a chicken. Liberians hoping to enter into such a relationship may address their potential patron with such words as, *Bossman, wa yu have fo me?* (Bossman, what you have for me?) "Sir, what do you have for me?"

**bounder**: [bãdɔ] *n.*, A scoundrel, a low-life. Old British slang. *Da bounder fini eat all my mar.* (That bounder finish eat all my mar.) "That low-life has run away with all my money."

**bra**: [bɹa] *n.*, Friend, buddy. Informal usage.

**break word**: [bɹekʼ wɔ] *v.*, To state one's opinion or judgment. *Wen de town elda dem meet to cut de case A will break word.* (When the town elder them meet to cut the case I will break word.) "I will give my opinion when the town elders meet to judge the case." See **hold word**.

**breeze**: [bɹis] *n.*, Used rather than "wind." *Las night, one heavy breeze carry de zinc.* (Last night one heavy breeze carry the zinc.) "Last night, a strong wind blew away the zinc roof."

**bright**: [bɹaɪ] *adj.*, Light skinned. A feature highly valued in Liberian culture. Contrasted with **black**. Note: The word *bright* is never heard in reference to someone's intelligence. For that see **cleva**. *Da bright geh too fine o!* (That bright girl too fine o!) "That light-skinned girl is very beautiful."

**broadcast**: [bɹakas] *v.*, To scatter widely, to sow. *De tam de farma wa broadcasting de see owa hih farm, de boid wa plenty behine heen.* (The time the farmer was broadcasting his seed over his farm, the bird was plenty behind him.) "When the farmer was sowing the seeds over his farm, there were a lot of birds following him."

**broken veins**: [bɹokẽ vẽs] *n.*, Stretch marks. *Ma Wata born ewasince, buh she stih geh broken veins on hur belly.* (Ma Wata born ever since, but she still get broken veins on her belly.) "Ma Wata gave birth a long time ago, but she still has stretch marks on her belly."

**brola**: [bɹəɾa] "brother" *n.*, 1. A rather loose term in Liberia that can refer to anyone from your actual brother to a friend, fellow tribesman, or mere acquaintance. *Ma brola to de packing na. A coming go mee heen.* (My brother to the packing now. I coming go meet him.) "My friend is at the bus station. I'm going to go meet him." 2. Title of respect commonly used in churches. *Brola James wa sick dis gone Sunay.* (Brother James was sick this gone Sunday.) "James was sick last Sunday."

**brush**: [bɹəʃ] *v.,* To clear vegetation with a cutlass. *A ain fini brushing de farm yeh.* (I ain't finish brushing the farm yet.) "I have not finished clearing the farm yet."

**buba**: [buba] *n.,* A long African gown. *De Mandingo dem luf to weh deh buba.* (The Mandingo them love to wear the buba.) "The Mandingos love to wear their long robes."

**bubbles**: [bəbos] *n.,* Illegal narcotics in the form of pills.

**buckeh**: [bʌkɛ] "bucket" *n.,* Used rather than "pail." *Ifan yu wan so A muh haul wata, yu muh show me wa play de buckeh ah.* (If you want so I must haul water, you must show me what place the bucket at.) "If you want me to carry water, you need to show me where the pail is."

**budduh wif**: [bʌdə wɪf] "butt up with" *v.,* To meet unintentionally, to run into. *Today A budduh wif one oh my old fren to de markeh.* (Today I butt up with one of my old friend to the market.) "I ran into an old friend at the market today."

**bugabug**: [bʌkʌbə] *n.,* Termite. Probably borrowed from the Malinke language *bagabaga.* There are many varieties of termites in Liberia, but the largest, *Macrotermes natalensis,* builds from clay large dome nests that dot the Liberian landscape. These can be more than ten feet tall. The large fatty queen found inside is eaten as a delicacy. The clay from these nests is often used to finish the exterior of mud-daubed houses. After the first rains, countless thousands of winged termite "scouts" fly, only a few of which will become queens of their own hills. The remaining mass of insects covers the landscape. They are collected by villagers and roasted for food. *De tam bugabug fly we going kesh some an roas ih.* (The time bugabug fly we going catch some and roast it.) "When the termites fly we will catch some to roast."

**bugabug eat your brain**: [bʌkʌbə i jo bɹaĩ] *idiom.,* A common insult, implies stupidity. *Wa happen yu na know da ting? Bugabug eat yo brain?* (What happen you not know that thing? Bugabug eat your brain?) "How do you not know that? Are you stupid?"

**buggar**: [bəga] *n.,* Casual reference to a man. Fellow, guy, etc. *Dis buggar yeh da my good fren.* (This buggar here that my good friend.) "This guy here is my good friend."

**bukar wee:** [bɔkɔ:wi] "bulgar wheat" *n.*, A food commonly distributed during the war in place of rice. Still available in local markets, but not preferred.

**bulleh-proof:** [bolɛ pɹof] "bullet-proof" *n.*, A fetish believed to prevent injury to the wearer when fired upon with a gun. *Da man wa having bulleh-proof. Dey fiya heen, buh ih ain do notting to heen.* (That man was wearing bullet proof. They fire him, but it ain't do nothing to him.) "That man had on a bullet-proof charm. They shot at him, but it didn't do anything to him."

**bunga:** [būga] *n.*, The buttocks. Slang usage.

**bungafish:** [būgafiʃ] *n.*, The vagina. Vulgar usage.

**bush:** [buʃ] 1. *n.*, Forest. *De hunta dem jus come fron een de bush.* (The hunter them just come from in the bush.) "The hunters just came back from the forest." 2. *n.*, Rural areas. *Da old ma na staylohn een de bush.* (That old ma now stay long in the bush.) "That old lady has lived in the countryside a long time." 3. *adj.*, Wild, from the forest. *A meh one bush cow on de road coming.* (I met one bush cow on the road coming.) "On the way here I came across a buffalo on the road."

**bush-bush:** [buʃ buʃ] *adj.*, Secretive, hushed. *Deh wa plenty bush-bush tok about Zuba woman palava.* (There was plenty bush bush talk about Zub woman palaver.) "There was a lot of hushed talk about Zuba's woman troubles."

**bush cat:** [buʃ kjæt˺] *n.*, Used in reference to a variety of feliform carnivores found in the forest including the genet (*Genetta spp.*), palm civet (*Nandinia binotata*), civit (*Civettictis civetta*) and Golden Cat (*Felis aurata*) *Da bush cat kill plenty chicken las night.* (That bush cat kill plenty chicken last night.) "That wild cat killed a lot of chickens last night."

**bush chicken:** [buʃ t͡ʃikī] *n.*, A term applied to several varieties of partridge. Considered a delicacy in Liberia. *A see one bush chicken on de ro today, buh A wa na having rubba gun to fiya ih.* (I see one bush chicken on the road today, but I was not having rubber gun to fire it.) "I saw a partridge on the road today, but I didn't have a slingshot to shoot it."

**bush cow:** [buʃ kau] *n.*, The West African Dwarf Buffalo. *Syncerus nanus.* The most common large mammal in Liberia. They often trample farms and cause great damage. Greatly feared for their sharp horns and aggressive temperament. *De bush cow dem fini spoil my farm.* (The bush cow them finish spoil my farm.) "Bush cows have ruined my farm."

**bush dog:** [buʃ dɔ] *n.*, The river otter. *Lutra maculicollis.* Brown with whitish underbelly. *Bush dog can spoil fish basket to eat de crab.* (Bush dog can spoil fish basket to eat the crab.) "Otters break open fish baskets to eat the crabs inside."

**bush goat**: [buʃ go] *n.,* The Black Duiker. *Cephalophus niger.* A dark brown or blackish forest antelope. *A been seeing one bush goat to my farm dee few tam.* (I been seeing one bush goat to my farm these few time.) "I've been seeing a black duiker on my farm recently."

**bush hog**: [buʃ hɔ] *n.,* A wild pig. The two common species in Liberia are the Giant Forest Hog, *Hylochoerus meinertzhageni,* and the Red River Hog, *Potamochoerus porcus.* Considered to be prime bush meat, although Muslim groups generally avoid it. *Yu muh tek tam befo de bush hog rooduh all yo cassava.* (You must take time before the bush hog root up all your cassava.) "You need to watch out or wild hogs will dig up all your cassava."

**bush meat**: [buʃ mi] *n.,* The meat of wild animals. Usually smoked. Generally preferred over domesticated meat. *A fising bush meat to sell to de markeh.* (I fixing bush meat to sell to the market.) "I'm preparing smoked game to sell in the market."

**bush rat**: [buʃ ɹæt'] *n.,* Refers to a variety of species of small wild rodents including the common dormouse.

**bush school**: [buʃ sku] *n.,* A function of the Poro and Sande power associations in which male and females are initiated as members into their respective societies. Adolescents are secluded in secret camps for a period of several weeks to several years and instructed in society matters. Initiates are marked with ritual scars. In the Sande bush, girls undergo female genital mutilation (FGM), commonly called "female circumcision" or "cutting". Upon completion, they are given a new name and presented to their families as adults. *Wa happing eenside de bush school no one will say.* (What happen inside the bush school no one will say.) "Nobody talks about what goes on in the bush schools. "

**bush taxi**: [buʃ tesi] *n.,* A colloquialism meaning to go on foot.

**bush wife**: [buʃ waif] *n.,* A woman from a rural area used by a city man for illicit sex. Can also refer to women used as sex slaves by rebels in the Liberian Civil War. *Een de war, de soya dem carry Mamee to be deh bush wife.* (In the war, the soldier them carry Mamee to be their bush wife.) "During the war, the soldiers captured Mamee to use as a sex slave."

**bush yam**: [buʃ jam] *n.,* A wild root vegetable. *Dioscorea prehensilis.* Although it is mildly toxic and the stems are covered in thorns, the roots may be gathered and eaten during times of scarcity. *De tam de war come,*

*we go hide een de bush an eat bush yam before we cu reesh Sierra Le-*
*one.* (The time the war come, we go hide in the bush and eat bush yam
before we could reach Sierra Leone.) "When the war came, we went and
hid in the forest and ate bush yams until we were able to get to Sierra
Leone." See **hungry food**.

**buss**: [bʌs] "bust" *v.*, 1. To break. *A meh doh pekin dem bussing palm kana*
*una de plum tree.* (I met those pekin them busting palm kernel under the
plum tree.) "I found those boys under the mango tree cracking open palm
kernels." 2. For rice grains to ripen on the stalk. *Rice cyan be bussing*
*tam lek dih.* (Rice can't be busting time like this.) "Rice doesn't ripen
this time of year." 3. To reveal a secret. *Gartee wa coming bus de society*
*secreh, so dey kill heen.* (Gartee was coming bust the society secret, so
they kill him.) "Gartee was about to reveal the society's secrets, so they
killed him."

**butta nose fish**: [bʌtʌ nos fiʃ] "butter nose fish" *n.*, The Threadfish. *Poly-*
*dactylus spp.* An ocean fish with a rounded nose. Commercially important in Liberia.

**butta pear**: [bʌtʌ pɛ] "butter pear" *n.*, The avocado. *Persea americana.*
*Butta pear can be swee wen yu eat ih wif vinega.* (Butter pear can be
sweet when you eat it with vinegar.) "Avocados are tasty when you eat
them with vinegar."

**butta rice**: [bʌtʌ ɹaɪs] "butter rice" *n.*, A popular variety of starchy rice
imported from China. *De butta rice too heavy. It can mek yu geh fat*
*quick quick.* (The butter rice too heavy. It can make you get fat quick
quick.) "Butter rice is very heavy. It can make you gain weight very
fast."

**buzzie**: [buzi] *n.*, A term used to refer to the **Lorma** ethnic group. Considered today to be pejorative.

**by an by**: [baɪ ã baɪ] *"by and by" adv.*, Used rather than "eventually." *De*
*baby wa too dry ah fwise, buh by an by she start getting betta.* (The baby
was too dry at first, but by and by she start getting better.) "The baby
was very dehydrated at first, but eventually she started getting better."

**by lan**: [bi lã] "by land" *adv.*, To go on foot. *He ain fine taxi, so he walk*
*by lan to go.* (He ain't find taxi, so he walk by land to go.) "He couldn't
find a taxi, so he went on foot."

# C

**cab moto**: [kæ moto] *n.*, A medium-sized truck. *A wan buy one cab moto so A can be hauling plank fron Bomi.* (I want buy one cab moto so I can be hauling plank from Bomi.) "I want to buy a truck to transport planks **from Bomi County.**"

**calabash**: [kælæbæʃ] n., Refers to gourds, mostly from the Calabash Tree. *Crescentia cujete.* Used in rural Liberia for sorting rice, carrying water, and making musical instruments.

**call me dog**: [kɔ mi dɔ] *idiom.*, An oath indicating that a person may be held in contempt if they fail to live up to their vow. *If A na bring de money yor can call me dog.* (If I not bring the money y'all can call me dog.) "If I don't bring the money you all can hold me in contempt."

**calopay**: [kalope] *n.*, A knockdown. Can be used in a metaphorical sense. *Who going gii da man calopay?* (Who going give that man calopay?) "Who is going to give that man a knockdown?"

**camo**: [kamo] "commode" *n.*, A toilet, lavatory. *Civilize man cyan toilet een de bush. He can use camo.* (Civilize man can't toilet in the bush. He can use commode.) "A civilized man doesn't defecate in the bush. He uses a toilet."

**cane juice**: [kẽ d͡ʒus] *n.*, A potent alcoholic beverage made from sugar cane. *Da de cane juice bisneh wa causing prorem een de village na.* (That the cane juice business what causing problem in the village now.) "Sugar cane liquor is the thing that's causing a lot of problems in the village now."

**car**: [ka:] *n.*, Used in a broader sense to refer to motorized vehicles bigger than a motorbike.

**car boy**: [ka: bɔɪ] *n.*, A young man who collects taxi or bus fares and loads the vehicles. Noted for the way they hang precariously on the back of fast-moving vehicles.

**careless greens**: [keles gɹĩs] *n.*, A variety of edible herb. *Amaranthus spp.* Most species blooms with a fuzzy and brightly-colored inflorescence. The leaves are used to make a sauce that is served over rice.

**car pay**: [ka: pe] *n.*, Taxi or bus fare. *A wa coming go to church yestuday, buh no car pay.* (I was coming go to church yesterday, but no car pay.) "I was planning on going to church yesterday, but I didn't have any money for a taxi."

**carry**: [kaɹi] *v.*, 1. To take. *Ma ole ma fini carry de pensil.* (My old ma finish carry the pestle.) "My grandma has taken the mortar pestle." 2. To

49

accompany. *A wan carry you on de ro.* (I want carry you on the road.) "I want to accompany you to the road." Note: Liberians usually do not use this word to mean physically carrying something. For this see **tote** and **haul**.

**cassava**: [kasava] *n.*, Manioc. *Manihot utilissima.* A staple crop of Liberia, especially in the south-east region. Native to South America but introduced during early European trade. The leaves are pounded, cooked, and eaten as a sauce over rice. The large tubors can be prepared in a number of ways. *A wan dig my cassava an mek it wif garee.* (I want dig my cassava and make it with garee.) "I want to harvest my cassava and make it into garee." See also **dumboy, GB, fufu, farina**, and **garee**.

**cassava fish**: [kasava fiʃ] *n.*, The Cassava Croaker. *Pseudotolithus senegalensis.* A medium-sized ocean fish. Covered in silvery scales. Important to local fishing industries.

**cassava leaf**: [kasava lif] *n.*, A sauce made from the leaves of the cassava plant. Served over rice. Also called **gbasa jamba**.

**cassava snek**: [kasava snɛk˺] *n.*, The Gabon viper. *Bites gabonica.* An extremely venomous snake with a large head and mottled brown coloration. A common treatment for hepatitis (**yellow janna**) in Liberia consists of drinking a broth made from a dried cassava snake. *De tam A wa coming fron my farm A budduh wif one cassava snek on de ro.* (The time I was coming from my farm I butt up with one cassava snake on the road.) "When I was coming from my farm I ran into a cassava snake on the path."

**cassette**: [kasɛ] *n.*, Used instead of "tape" when referring to audio cassettes. See **tape**.

**cat eye**: [kiæt˺ aɪ] *n.*, Used to describe eye color lighter than the dark brown usual for Liberians. *Finda da cat eye geh deh.* (Finda that cat eye girl there.) "Finda is that girl with the light brown eyes."

**catguh**: [kiægə] "cat gut" *n.*, Nylon fishing line. *A wan buy some catguh so A can fishing.* (I want buy some cat gut so I can fishing.) "I want to buy some fishing line so I can go fishing."

**catoon**: [katũ:] *n.*, A cardboard box, carton. For animated films see **Mickey Mouse show**. *A can plea carry dis ole catoon?* (I can please carry this old carton?) "Could I please take this old box?"

**cause noise**: [kɔz noɪs] *v.*, To make a racket, be noisy. *Dee children dem love causing plenty noise.* (These children them love causing plenty noise.) "These children like making a lot of noise." See also **hala-hala**.

**cauz**: [kɔz] "curse" *v.*, To insult, to verbally abuse. *Why yu wan cauz me so?* (Why you want curse me so?) "Why do you want to insult me like that?" See also **abuse**.

**cavally**: [kavali] *n.*, The Atlantic Horse Mackerel. Important to the local fishing industry. *Trachurus trachurus.* From the Portuguese language.

**chakla**: [t͡ʃakla] 1. *v.*, To mess up, to leave in a state of disorder. Possibly from the Ewe language. *Doh chicken fini chackla de play!* (Those chicken finish chackla the place!) "Those chickens messed up the place!" 2. *adj.*, To mess up. *Eryting chakla deh.* (Everything chakla there.) "Everything is all messed up there." 3. *v.*, To scatter, go in separate directions. Uncommon usage. *Leh we eat small somting, den we all going chackla.* (Let we eat small something, then we all going chackla.) "Let's eat something and then go our separate ways."

**chamt**: [t͡ʃamt˺] "chant" *v.*, Refers to the recitation of a portion of the Koran for magical purposes. See **moliman**.

**charm**: [t͡ʃaːm] *v.*, To use a magical spell. *Da man charm de chief befo he geh da position.* (That man charm the chief before he get that position.) "That man cast a spell on the chief in order to get that position."

**ché**: [t͡ʃé] *interj.*, An expression of surprise. *Ché! Liverpool win Chelsea?* (Che! Liverpool win Chelsea?) "What? Liverpool beat Chelsea?"

**cheche**: [t͡ʃet͡ʃe] *n.*, Gossip. *Soon ah A leave dey can start toking cheche behine me.* (Soon as I leave they can start talking cheche behind me.) "As soon as I leave they start to share gossip about me behind my back."

**chechepolay**: [t͡ʃet͡ʃepole] *n.*, A busybody, a gossip. *Da chechepolay muh leave my name.* (That chechepolay must leave my name.) "That gossip should stop talking about me." See also **besse** and **gehdah**.

**check**: [t͡ʃɛk˺] *v.*, To apply, squeeze (in referece to brakes). *De tam yu coming don de hill on yo motobike, yu muh na check yo fron brake so yu muh na fall don.* (The time you coming down the hill on your motorbike, you must not check your front brake so you must not fall down.) "To avoid falling, when you are going down a hill on your motorbike, you should not use your front brakes."

**check rice**: [t͡ʃɛk˺ ɹaɪs] *n.*, A rice dish with chopped greens mixed in.

**chext**: [t͡ʃɛkst˺] *n.*, A common pronunciation of "chest".

**chext co**: [t͡ʃɛkst˺ ko] "chest cold" *n.*, A respiratory infection. More serious than a **fresh co**.

**chicken hawk**: [t͡ʃikẽ hɔk˺] *n.*, A kind of raptor known for swooping down and catching chickens.

**chicken rogue**: [tʃikē rog] *n.*, Someone known for stealing chickens. *Dey flok da pekin goo goo wen de fineoh da he de chicken rogue.* (They flog that pekin good good when they find out that he the chicken rogue.) "They gave that boy a good beating when they found out that he was the chicken thief."

**chicken soup**: [tʃikē su] *n.*, Bullion cubes. Added to Liberian sauces for flavor. *De chicken soup na plenty agin.* (The chicken soup not plenty again.) "The bullion cubes are running out."

**chief**: [tʃif] *n.*, 1. A traditional tribal leader. See **paramount chief, clan chief, town chief** and **nyoung boy chief**. 2. An honorific title used loosely for any person of influence. See also **bossman**.

**chiefdom**: [tʃifdɔ̄] *n.*, A political unit, under the district level. Made up of territory primarily inhabited by people in the same extended clan or closely related clans.

**chigga**: [tʃɪgə] *n.*, see **jigga**

**chop**: [tʃap] 1. *n.*, Food. *A fini buy de chop.* (I finish buy the chop.) "I have bought the food." 2. *v.*, To eat. *A coming go chop na.* (I coming go chop now.) "I'm going to eat now." 3. *v.*, To consume money or resources. *All oh yor tink yor going be chopping fron dis lil piece oh job?* (All of y'all think y'all going be chopping from this little piece of job?) "Do all of you think you're going to make money off this one little job?"

**chopier**: [tʃapiɛ] *n.*, see **whipper**.

**chunk**: [tʃʌkˈ] 1. *v.*, To throw, hurl. *Chunk da ball na!* (Chunk the ball now!) "Throw the ball now!" 2. *v.*, This word does not require an object and can stand alone to mean, "to throw an object." *Yu muh na chunk yo fren, yeh!* (You must not chunk your friend, you hear!) "You should not throw things at your friend!"

**church moda**: [tʃɔʃ mʌda] "church mother" *n.*, An older lady in a church who serves as the backbone for the congregation, and is the primary women's leader. *Ma Lorpu, da she de church moda yah.* (Mrs. Lorpu, that she the church mother here.) "Mrs. Lorpu is the church mother here."

**civilize**: [sɪvɪlaɪ] "civilized" *adj.*, Westernized, Christianized, educated. Because of the pseudo-colonial history of Liberia, many Liberians believe Western culture to be superior to traditional African culture. Thus to say someone is not civilized is a grave insult. *Dis yo fren yeh ain civilize.* (This your friend here ain't civilize.) "Your friend here is not Westernized" See also **kwi**.

**citizen**: [sɪtɪsẽ] *n.*, Townspeople. While this term can apply to national citizenship, it is commonly heard in reference to the native inhabitants of a town or county. *Fo long de Totota citizen dem been coming to Gbarnga fo markeh.* (For long the Totota citizen them been coming to Gbarnga for market.) "For a long time the residents of Totota have been coming to Gbarnga to buy and sell in the market."

**city**: [sɪti] *n.*, A community populated by more than several thousand people, containing a large central market, packing station, schools, etc. Beyond Monrovia, most other places in Liberia referred to as cities would be considered towns by Standard English speakers. See also **town**.

**clan**: [klã] *n.*, A political unit consisting of a section of a chiefdom. Membership in a clan does not necessarily imply common decent. Because of geographic isolation, many clans speak a unique dialect of their larger language group.

**clan chief**: [klã t͡ʃif] *n.*, The leader of the clan. Represents the interests of the clan in local governments. This position is determined in some cases by descent, but more commonly through political means of campaigning and election.

**clear bush**: [kli buʃ] *v.*, See **clean farm**.

**clean farm**: [klĩ fa:m] *v.*, To cut underbrush in preparation for planting. See also **scrash farm** and **boin farm**.

**coat-suit**: [ko su] *n.*, A two or three-piece suit. Commonly worn for church services or other special occasions.

**co bo**: [ko:bo] "cold bowl" *n.*, Left-over food. *Ifan yu ain wan kesh running stomac, yu muh warm yo co bo goo befo eating ih.* (If you ain't want catch running stomach, you must warm your cold bowl good before eating it.) "If you don't want to get diarrhea, you should heat your leftovers well before eating them."

**co bo shop**: [ko:bo ʃa] "cold bowl shop" *n.*, See **cookshop**.

**cobraheh**: [kobɹahɛ] "cobra head" *n.*, Slang term for a popular inexpensive cellphone with a shape reminiscent of a cobra's open hood. Also known as **bonanza**.

**coffee bag fall een de wata**: [kɔfi be fɔ ĩ dɛ wata] "coffee bag fall in the water" *idiom.*, A humorous expression meaning 'to loose one's mind'. *Don mine da guy. Hih coffee bag fall een de wata.* (Don't mind that guy. His coffee bag fall in the water.) "Never mind that guy. He's out of his mind."

**cohpa**: [kʊpa] "cookpot" *n.*, A pot used for cooking. Generally made from cast iron or aluminum. *Wen yu fini cooking de rice, yu muh plea wash de* *cohpa, yah?* (When you finish cooking the rice, you must please wash the cookpot, you hear?) "When you finish cooking the rice please wash the pot, OK?"

**cohsha**: [kuʃa] "cookshop" *n.*, A simple restaurant selling African foods. *Hand to Mouth cohsha can fis GB pa all de ola cohsha dem.* (Hand to Mouth cookshop can fix GB past all the other cookshop them.) "Hand to Mouth cookshop makes the best GB around."

**cohspoon**: [kuspū] "cook-spoon" n., A large metal spoon used in cooking. *De kalla fini doning. Tek de cohspoon an move ih fron de oil.* (The kalla finish doning. Take the cook spoon and move it from the oil.) "The doughnuts are done cooking. Use the cooking spoon to remove them from the oil."

**colleh**: [kolɛ] "collect" *v.*, To retrieve, to pick up. *Wen A fini to de markeh A coming colleh de chiren to de school.* (When I finish to the market I coming collect the children to the school.) "When I am done in the market I am going to pick up the kids at school."

**colloma**: [koloma] 1. *adj.*, Fake, imitation. 2. *n.*, Something that is fake, an imitation, a lie. *A tell heen to bring de real Nike skubee buh he bring de colloma own.* (I tell him to bring the real Nike skubee but he bring the colloma own.) "I told him to bring genuine Nike sneakers but he brought imitations."

**color**: [kələ] *n.*, The African-American accent. Often spoken by Liberians returning from the States, although doing so may be considered by others to be pretentious. *Gayflor come fron de US. Na he toking color.* (Gayflor come from the US. Now he talking color.) "Gayflor came from the US. Now he is talking like an African-American."

**come down**: [kʌ̃ dã] *v.*, To get off a vehicle. *A wan come down Reh Light.* (I want come down Red Light.) "I want to get off at Red Light." See also **drop**.

**coming**: kʌmī] *v.*, 1. The incompletive aspect marker. *A coming go Gbarnga tomorrow.* (I coming go Gbarnga tomorrow.) "I am going to go to Gbarnga tomorrow." 2. The phrase *A coming.* "I'm coming" is used to mean "hold on," "wait a minute," etc.

**come leh eat**: [kʌ̃ lɛ itˀ] "Come let's eat," *verb phrase.*, A mandatory invitation that is always extended if a person is eating and their friend arrives.

**common**: [kamɔ̃] *adj.*, Well known. *If yu know book, dis ting shu be common to yu.* (If you know book, this thing should be common to you.) "If you are educated, this thing should be well known to you."

**comping:** [kɔŋpiŋ] "company" *n.,* A rotational savings club. Members put money into a pool from which they borrow in turn. More commonly called **kuu** or **susu**.

**complain:** [kãplãĩ] "complaint" *n.,* A problem (usually physical.) *Ma chext geh serious complain. A wan go see de docta.* (My chest get serious complaint. I want go see the doctor.) "I have a serious problem with my chest. I want to see the doctor. "

**Congo:** [kɔŋgo] *adj.,* The freed slaves who settled in Liberia. Originally applied to those from captured slave vessels from Central Africa who were off-loaded in Liberia, but later applied to the Americo-Liberian settlers as well. This term is considered somewhat pejorative. *Settler* is a more neutral term used to refer to the same people. *Some of de country peepo use to sen deh chiren dem to be living wif de Congo peepo so dey could be civilize.* (Some of the country people used to send their children them to be living with the Congo people so they could be civilized.) "Some of the indigenous people used to send their children to live with the Congo people so they could learn Western customs."

**congosa:** [cõngosa] *n* 1. *n.,* A rumor-monger, gossip. See also **besse, chechepolay** and **gehdah.** 2. *v.,* To spread gossip.

**conniving:** [kãnivĩ] *v.,* 1. To plot something in secret. *A hope yor all muh na be conniving behine me.* (I hope you all must not be conniving behind me.) "I hope you all are not plotting something behind my back." 2. To commit adultery. *De tam A reesh to de hus A fine oh da my woman been conniving.* (The time I reach to the house I find out that my woman been conniving.) "When I got to my house I found out that my wife had been committing adultery."

**copa:** [ko:pa] "coal pot" *n.,* A raised iron grill used to cook food over charcoal. *De blacksmif fini fising my copa.* (The blacksmith finish fixing my coal pot.) "The blacksmith already made my coal pot."

**correc:** [koɹɛ] *adj.,* Very good, high-quality, without any problems. *Da de correc tape dih.* (That the correct tape this.) "This is a very good cassette player."

**corner-corner:** [kɔ̃nakɔ̃na] *adj.,* Corrupt. See **krokroji**.

**cotar:** [kota:] "coal tar" *n.,* An asphalt road. *De Monrovia cotar na rough pa de Lofa road.* (The Monrovia coal tar now rough past the Lofa road.) "The paved roads in Monrovia are worse now than the dirt road to Lofa County."

**cottor:** [kotɔ] *n.,* 1. A piece of cloth rolled in a circle and used to balance a load on one's head. *Plea borrow me yo handkerchief so A can use ih fo cottor.* (Please borrow me your handkerchief so I can use it for cotto.)

"Please lend me your handkerchief so I can use it to carry something on my head." 2. A tourniquet. *Snek boin me, so A tie cottor on my foot.* (Snake burn me, so I tie cotto on my foot.) "A snake bit me, so I tied a tourniquet on my leg."

**cotton tree**: [katɛ̃ t͡ʃɹi] *n.,* The Silk Cotton Tree. *Bombax costatum.* A thorny tree commonly found near villages in their Poro groves. Named for the cotton-like seeds that are carried by the wind. Traditionally believed to be the dwelling place of forest spirits. *Dey wa waning to cut da cotton tree, buh de jina wa wa eenside ain agree, so dey cun abo ih.* (They was wanting to cut that cotton tree, but the jina what was inside ain't agree, so they couldn't able it.) "They were wanting to cut down that cotton tree, but the spirits living in the tree did not consent, so they weren't able to do it."

**country**: [kɔ̃t͡ʃɹi] *adj.,* 1. Traditional, pertaining to rural life. 2. When used in reference to people this word has negative connotations. *Da country boy ain know book.* (That country boy ain't know book.) "That country bumpkin isn't educated."

**country breh**: [kɔ̃tɹɛ bɹɛ] "country bread" *n.,* Pounded rice meal, usually made from newly harvested rice. Eaten raw on the farm or on long treks. Also has ritualistic uses in offerings to the ancestral spirits. See **also nyew rice**.

**country cloh**: [kɔ̃tɹɛ klɔ] "country cloth" *n.,* Local woven cloth. Used to make the colorful gowns worn by chiefs.

**country chalk**: [kɔ̃tɹɛ t͡ʃɔk˺] *n.,* A white clay. Some tribes value it as a nutritional supplement and will actually eat it. It can also be used for medicine or ritualistic purposes. Also known as **potta**. *De tam de geh dem come fron de Sande bush, dey going be all cowa een country chalk.* (The time the girl them come from the Sande bush, they going be all cover in country chalk.) "When the girls come out of the Sande bush, they will be covered in white clay."

**country chicken**: [kɔ̃tɹɛ t͡ʃikĩ] *n.,* Refers to the local variety of chicken. Generally smaller and tougher than common Western varieties. *Yu looking dry lek one country chicken.* (You looking dry like one country chicken.) "You look as skinny as a village chicken."

**country chop**: [kʌ̃tri t͡ʃɔp] *n.,* A dish consisting of stewed meats and fish. Served with rice. It is often garnished with hard-boiled eggs, coconut and fruit .

**country docta**: [kɔ̃tɹɛ data] "country doctor" *n.,* A traditional healer. See also zoe and **sick bush**.

**country guita**: [kɔtɹɛ gɪta] "country guitar" *n.*, A general term for home-made stringed instruments. One common variety is made from raffia stems and has a soundbox and a neck resembling a Western guitar. *Da boy to Kollie's town fis one country guita dee few days.* (That boy to Kollie's town fix one country guitar these few days.) "That boy in Kollie's town made a country guitar recently."

**country medicine**: [kɔtɹɛ mɛɾasĩ] "country medicine" *n.*, Traditional African herbal remedies. *De docta cyan do noting fo me agin. A coming go fine some country medicine.* (The doctor can't do nothing for me again. I coming go find some country medicine.) "The doctor can't do any more for me. I am going to find some traditional medicine."

**country money**: [kɔtɹɛ mʌne] *n.*, Twisted metal rods formerly traded as currency in northwestern Liberia. Usually between 12-18 inches in length. May still be found for sale in souvenir shops in Monrovia.

**country rice**: [kɔtɹɛ ɹaɪs] "country rice" *n.*, Rice locally grown and hulled by being pounded in a mortar. *Country rice sweet pa butta rice, buh ih cyan mek ih wif co bo.* (Country rice sweet past butter rice, but it can't make it with cold bowl.) "Country rice is tastier than butter rice, but it doesn't make good left-overs."

**country rope**: [kɔtɹɛ ɹop] *n.*, Forest vines used to tie things. *De tam Mulbah coming fron de farm, A wan so he muh bring some country rope.* (The time Mulbah coming from the farm, I want so he must bring some country rope.) "I want Mulbah to bring some vines when he is coming back from the farm."

**country salt**: [kɔtɹɛ sal] *n.*, Refers to a potash or soda made from the ashes of the leaves of palm tree, plantain, and certain wild grasses. A popular flavoring agent in Lofa County. See also **torbagee**.

**country wife**: [kɔtɹɛ waɪf] *n.*, Refers to an indigenous women married in the traditional tribal fashion to a **kwi** man. See also **traditional marriage**.

**country zinc**: [kɔtɹɛ zĩ] *n.*, See **papu**.

**county**: [kãti] *n.*, The major administrative divisions of Liberia. They include Montserrado, Margibi Grand Cape Mount, Gbarpolu, Bomi, Grand Bassa, Sino, Maryland, River Gee, Grand Kru, Lofa, Bong, and Nimba. These are further divided into districts, clans and townships.

**co wata (1)**: [ko wata] "cold water" *n.*, A little bit of money. A bribe. A gift to "grease the wheels." *Yu can plea help me wif small cold water?* "You can please help me with small cold water?") "Could you please give me a little money?"

**co wata (2):** [ko wata] "cold water" *adj.*, From the ocean. *My ma bought one big co wata catfish fron de fisherman.* (My ma bought one big cold water catfish from the fisherman.) "My mother bought a big ocean catfish from the fisherman."

**co wata (3):** [ko wata] "cold water" *n.*, Slang for alcohol.

**crackay:** [kɹake] "crack head" *adj.*, Stubborn, argumentative, insolent. *Da crackay pekin rally love palava.* (That crackay pekin really love palaver.) "That stubborn kid really loves to stir up trouble."

**crawcraw (1):** [kɹakɹa] *n.*, Scabies. A very common skin problem for children in rural Liberia. *Dis crawcraw been giving my baby hard tam.* (This crawcraw been giving my baby hard time.) "My baby has been having a lot of problems from scabies."

**crawcraw (2):** [kɹawkɹaw] *n*, A colloquial term for the most common variety of peanut.

**crawfish:** [kɹɔfiʃ] *n.*, A prawn. Shrimp-like crustaceans common in Liberian streams and rivers. Caught in baskets and eaten in soups. *Crawfish sweet pa boney een palm butta.* (Crawfish sweet past boney in palm butter.) "Crawfish are tastier than dried fish in palm butter sauce."

**craw-craw frog:** [kɹakɹa fɹa] *n.*, A toad. *Buffo spp.* It is commonly believed that the warty skin of toads can cause scabies. *We can eat spring frog, buh dog sef cyan eat craw-craw frog.* (We can eat spring frog, but dog self can't eat craw-craw frog.) "We eat spring frogs, but even dogs don't eat toads."

**crazy man:** [kɹesi mɛ̃] *n.*, A lunatic, insane person, someone who is out of his mind. Often used to refer to mentally unstable persons who wander the streets. *Deh geh one crazy man to Salala wa can sleep to de markeh.* (They get one crazy man to Salala what can sleep to the market.) "There is an insane person in Salala who sleeps in the market."

**credih:** [kɹɛdɪ] "credit" 1. *v.*, To loan, advance money. *Eh ba, yu muh plea credih me small somting.* (Eh ba, you must please credit me small something.) "Hey buddy, you have to lend me a little something." 2. *n.*, Units or minutes on a cell phone. *A wa coming call yu buh my credih fini.* (I was coming call you but my credit finish.) "I was going to call you, but I ran out of minutes."

**crush:** [kɹʌʃ] *v.*, To have romantic feelings for someone. *De chiren say da Eunice is crushing Jacob.* (The children say that Eunice is crushing Jacob.) "The kids say that Eunice has a crush on Jacob."

**cruss:** [kɹɔ] "crust" *n.*, Rice crust. The toasted crust that forms on the sides of the pot. Considered to be delicious. *Wen A fini dishing oh de rice A* *will leh de chiren eat de cruss.* "When I finish dishing out the rice I will let the children eat the crust."

**cuhbor**: [kʌbɔ] "cupboard" *n.*, Used rather than "cabinet."

**culture**: [kɔʃa] *n.*, This word in Liberia almost always refers to the traditional secret societies and related esoteric activities. *Yu cyan tok notting agins doh peepo culture bisneh.* (You can't talk nothing against those people culture business.) "You can't say anything against those people's secret society." See also **devil bush** and **poro**.

**cup**: [kʌp] *n.*, 1. The standard unit of measurement for rice. Equivalent to about 15 ounces. 2. A small can. Commonly sold canned items include tomato paste, sardines and mackerel. *Yu muh buy two tomato cup fo de soup.* (You must buy two tomato cup for the soup.) "You should buy two cans of tomato paste for the sauce."

**curren**: [kuɹẽ] "current" *n.*, Electricity. *De curren cut, so no light tonight.* (The current cut, so no light tonight.) "The electricity cut off, so there is no light tonight."

**cut**: [kʌt'] 1. *v.*, To stall. *A wa climbing de hill wen my motobike engine cut.* (I was climbing the hill when my motorbike engine cut.) "When I was climbing the hill my motorbike stalled." 2. *v.*, To turn off something. *Yu muh plea cut off de li, yah?* (You must please cut off the light, you hear?) "Won't you please turn off the light?" 3. *v.*, To cut off, remove. *Hih leg cut een de war.* (His leg cut in the war.) "He lost his leg in the war." 4. *v.*, To judge a case. *Dey go to de nyoung boy chief to cut de case.* (They go to the young boy chief to cut the case.) "They went to the village youth leader to judge the case." 5. *v.*, To perform clitoridectomy in the Sande bush. *Solong de zoe ain cut hur, she ain real woman.* (So long the zoe ain't cut her, she ain't real woman.) "If the zoe doesn't circumcise her, she will not be a real woman." 6. *v.*, To divide or distribute. *Yor cut de rice yeh?* (Y'all cut the rice yet?) "Did you all divide the rice yet?" 7. *v.*, To harvest. *De dry season na com. We coming cut rice soon.* (The dry season now come. We coming cut rice soon.) "The dry season is here. We are going to harvest rice soon."

**cutlax**: [kʌlaks] *n.*, A machete. *Wen A fini sharping de cutlax A going cut stick.* (When I finish sharping the cutlass I going cut stick.) "When I'm done sharpening the machete I will cut down some branches."

**cycle**: [sikɔ] *n.*, Bicycle. *He carry hih cycle een town?* (He carry his cycle in town?) "Did he take his bike to town?"

# D

**dammih**: [dæmɪ] "damn it" *interj.*, A common expression of surprise or agreement. Not considered vulgar as in Standard English.

**dandy jack**: [dãdi d͡ʒæk˺] *n.*, The Diana Monkey. *Cercopithecus diana diana.* A large black and red monkey with a distinctive white beard. Also called **king monkey**.

**dash** (1): [dæʃ] *v.*, To throw hastily towards the ground. *Wen he fini sucking de orange, he going dash ih don.* (When he finish sucking the orange, he going dash it down.) "When he is done sucking the juice out of the orange, he will throw it down."

**dash** (2): [dæʃ] *n.*, A gratuity directed from the seller to the buyer, a lagniappe. *De way yu buy de ten okra A coming gii noda one fo dash.* (The way you buy the ten okra, I coming give another one for dash.) "Because you bought the ten okras, I will give you another one as a bonus."

**day boy**: [de bɔɪ] *n.*, A casual laborer hired on a day to day basis. *Plenty day boy dem can be to Freeport een de morning looking fo small piece oh job.* (Plenty day boy them can be to Freeport in the morning looking for small piece of job.) "Lot of casual laborers meet by Freeport in the morning looking for a little work."

**daybreak**: [debɹek˺] *n.*, Used rather than "dawn" or "sunrise." *Soon ah daybreak come we can be going to de farm.* (Soon as daybreak come we can be going to the farm.) "As soon as dawn comes we go to the farm."

**dealing**: [dilĩ] *v.*, To use witchcraft for a desired end. *Da man dealing. Da wa mek ih he sucessful een hih bisneh.* (That man dealing. That what make it he successful in his business.) "That man is using witchcraft. That's why he is successful in his business."

**dear**: [diɛ] *adj.*, Expensive. Borrowed from the British usage. *Tomato too dear na.* (Tomato too dear now.) "Tomatoes are very expensive now."

**dee few days**: [di fiu des] "these few days" *adj.*, Used rather than "recently." *Ih been raining too much dee few days.* (It been raining too much these few days.) "It's been raining a lot recently."

**dee few tam**: [di fiu tã] "these few time" *adj.*, See **dee few days**.

**deep**: [dip] *adj.*, Difficult, profound, relating to ancient traditions. *Da ole man speak de deep Bassa, awa own pa miss uh wif too mush oh English.* (That old man speak the deep Bassa; our own part mix up with too much of English.) "That old man speaks the old Bassa language; as for us, ours has a lot of English mixed inside."

**deepa**: [dipa] "deeper" *n.*, A deep pool of calm water in an otherwise fast moving stream or river. Popularly believed to be the abode of dangerous creatures and water spirits. *Dey geh some ba ba jina wa can be living in dis deepa.* (They get some bad bad jina what can be living in this deeper.) "There are dangerous spirits living in this pool."

**deepot**: [dipɔ] *n.*, A dough made of reconstituted cassava flakes. *Fo me na, deepot na sweet lek GB* (For me now, deepot not sweet like GB.) "As far as I am concerned, deepot is not as tasty as GB" See also **GB**.

**deer**: [diɛ] *n.*, A duiker or antelope. Common throughout Liberia's forest and farmlands. *Reh deer ain sweet lek ans bear.* (Red deer ain't sweet like ants bear.) "Red duiker meat isn't as tasty as pangolin."

**deh**: [dɛ] "There" *adv.*, To simply exist or get by. *We jus deh.* (We just there.) "We're just getting by."

**deh body**: [de badi] "dead body" *n.*, Used rather than "corpse." *Dey fini carry de deh body to de funeral home.* (They finish carry the dead body to the funeral home.) "They already carried the body to the funeral home."

**deku**: [deku] *n.*, A lazy person who only pretends to work.

**dem**: [dɛ̃] "them" 1. An associative plural marker meaning "and the others." *Yu see George dem een town?* (You see George them in town?) "Did you see George and the others in town?" 2. Plural marker. Since Liberians often use nouns only in their singular form, *dem* is used to indicate plurality. *De dog dem can alway be on de car ro.* (The dog them can always be on the car road.) "The dogs are always on the car road."

**den**: [dɛ̃] "than" *conj.*, Used in comparisons. *Patrice tall den Janet.* (Patrice tall than Janet.) "Patrice is taller than Janet." See also **pa**.

**de tam**: [de tã] "the time" *adv.*, Often used rather than "when" and "while." *Da de tam A wa coming beep yu, buh my credih fini.* (That the time I was coming beep you, but my credit finish.) "That's when I was going to beep you, but the units on my phone had run out."

**deuce**: [dus] 1. *v.*, To ace, to perform well on an exam. *Jackson deuce de biology tes.* (Jackson deuce the biology test.) "Jackson aced the biology test." 2. *n.*, The top of one's class. The valedictorian. *Paul wa de deuce oh hih class.* (Paul was the deuce of his class.) "Paul was at the top of his class."

**devil**: [dɛwo] *n.*, Masked dancer, associated with the Poro and Sande secret societies. Not to be confused with Satan of the Christian or Islamic tradition. Devils in Liberia are not considered evil, but simply very powerful. They speak with a strange, throaty voice in a secret language known only to a handful of people in the **Poro**. *Wen de devil come fron een de bush, yor wa ain een de Poro muh go eenside yo hus befo he kesh yu!* (When the devil come from in the bush, y'all what ain't in the Poro must go inside your house before he catch you!) "When the masked dancer comes from the sacred grove, you all who aren't Poro members should go in your house so he doesn't catch you."

**devil bisneh**: [dɛwo bɪnɪ] *n.*, Affairs relating to the Poro or Sande.

**devil bush**: [dɛwo buʃ] *n.*, 1. The Poro and Sande societies. *De Muslim dem can rally kesh hard tam fron de devil bush.* (The Muslim them can really catch hard time from the devil bush.) "The Muslims faces a lot of opposition from the Poro society." See also **bush school**. 2. The meeting place of the Poro and Sande societies.

**devil interpreter**: [dɛwo ĩtɛɹpɹɛtɔ] *n.*, A high-ranking member of the Poro society who interprets the speech of the masked dancers.

**de way**: [dɛ we] "the way" *conj.*, Because. *De way A fini come soon, A going do mo work today.* (The way I finish come soon, I going do more work today.) "Because I have arrived early, I will do a lot of work today."

**Dey**: [de] *n.*, A small ethnic group of about 8,000 people living on the coastal region of western Liberia. Also known as the Dewe or Dewoi. They speak a language in the Kwa family related to Bassa. Although once a powerful tribe, the Dey are being gradually assimilated by the Gola and Vai. Majority Muslim.

**dey say**: [de se] "they say" *n.*, Rumors, second-hand information, gossip. *Da so so dey say A been yehing.* (That so so they say I been hearing.) "It's only rumors I've been hearing."

**didiba**: [didiba] *n.*, Deceit, trickery. See **krokroji**.

**diffren-diffren**: [dɪfɹɛ̃ dɪfɹɛ̃] "different-different" *adj.*, Varied, many kinds. *Dey geh diffren-diffren shop to Water Side.* (They get different-different shop to Water Side.) "There are many different kinds of shops in the Water Side Market."

**dilek**: [daɪlɛk] "dialect" *n.*, An indigenous African language. There are seventeen officially recognized native languages in Liberia. *Da man cyan abo to tok hih owna dilek sef!* (That man can't able to talk his own of dialect self!) "That man doesn't even know how to speak his own tribe's language!"

**dingo**: [dɪŋgo] *n.*, A pejorative reference to the Mandingo ethnic group.

**dis coming**: [dɪs kʌmĩ] "this coming" *adj.* Used in reference to days of the week to mean the next stated day, whether this week or the next. *De drill will be dis coming Wednesday.* (The drill will be this coming Wednesday.) "The parade will be this Wednesday."

**dis gone**: [dɪs gɔ̃] "this gone" *adj.* This past. Used in reference to days of the week. *A kill plenty fish dis gone Friday.* (I kill plenty fish this gone Friday). "I killed a lot of fish this past Friday"

**dishcloh**: [dɪʃ klɔ] "dishcloth" *n.,* Eczema. A skin condition characterized by rash, itchiness and a change in pigmentation. *Ma son having dishcloh on hih heh, so A coming carry heen to de clinih.* (My son having dishcloth on his head, so I coming carry him to the clinic.) "My son has eczema on his head, so I am taking him to the clinic."

**distance**: [dɪstã] *n.,* Commonly used rather than "long way" or "far" in discussing travel time. *Yu wan go fron yeh Belle Fassama? Da distance o!* (You want go from here Belle Fassama? That distance o!) "You want to go from here to Belle Fassama? That's a very long trip!" Contrasted with **na far**.

**district**: [dɪstɹɪ] *n.,* A political divisions under the county level. The borders often occur on tribal or clan boundaries and each district may contain several chiefdoms. Districts are governed by an elected district commissioner.

**distup**: [dɪstɔp] "disturb" 1. *v.,* To ruin, devastate. *De grasscutta distup my swam rice.* (The grasscutter disturb my swamp rice.) "The cane rats have devastated my swamp rice." 2. *adj.,* Used rather than upset, anxious, troubled, etc. *A wa distup de tam dey tell me say de ole ma loss een de bush.* (I was disturb the time they tell me say the old ma lost in the bush.) "I was troubled when they told me the old lady was lost in the forest."

**dite**: [daɪt˺] "dirt." *n.,* Garbage, refuse, trash. *A ain luf to see plenty dite een my yar.* (I ain't love to see plenty dirt in my yard.) "I don't like to see a lot of garbage in my yard."

**divide**: [dɪvaɪd] *v.,* To pass out, distribute, share. *Dey fini divide de issue, buh me pa, A ain receive.* (They finish divide the issue, but my part, I ain't receive.) "They distributed the goods, but as for me, I didn't get any."

**Doe dala**: [do dala] "Doe dollar" *n.,* The system of currency instituted under President Samuel Doe in the 1980s. The coins still carry some commercial value in rural markets. Replaced by the **Liberty** dollar.

**dog fish**: [dɔ fɪʃ] *n.,* See **lepor fish**.

**dogafleh**: [dɔgaflɛ] *n.*, Refers to second-hand clothes imported from the US. Often sold in piles on the ground. From a Kpelle phrase meaning "bend down market." *Wen A money man A will buy my clo fron de fine fine store dem on Broad Street. Untih den da dogafleh A will be wearing.* (When I money man I will buy my clothes from the fine fine store them on Broad Street. Until then that dogafleh I will be wearing.) "When I am a rich man I will buy my clothes from the fancy stores on Broad Street. Until then I will wear second-hand clothes.)

**doll baby**: [dɔ bebi] *n.*, Used instead of "baby doll." In rural areas parents often make simple dolls for their daughters from raffia fronds with hair made from oil palm fiber. *A geh fine doll baby fo yo, lil geh.* (I get fine doll baby for you, little girl.) "I have a beautiful baby doll for you, little girl."

**dolphin fish**: *n.*, Mahi-mahi. *Coryphaena hippurus*. A species of ocean fish highly prized for its tasty flesh.

**don**: [dõ] "don't" *adv.*, Also used for doesn't and didn't. Negates clauses. The initial [d] is often dropped and the word pronounced "on" [õ]. *Da man say he don wan go Monrovia.* (That man say he don't want go Monrovia.) "That man said he doesn't want to go to Monrovia."

**done**: [dʌ̃] *v.*, To be finished cooking. *De bukar wee fini doning jus na.* (The bulgur wheat finish doning just now.) "The bulgur wheat has just finished cooking." See also **fini**.

**donfa**: [dõfa] *n.*, A duck. *Donfa ma can mine her chiren pa chicken ma.* (Donfa ma can mind her children past chicken ma.) "Mother ducks watch their ducklings more carefully than mother chickens watch their chicks."

**doodoo boid**: [dudu bɔɪd] "doodoo bird" *n.*, The Senegal Coucal, *Centropus senegalensis*. A medium sized, low flying bird. Brown and white in color. Commonly seen in the brushland around towns and villages. The calls of the bird are believed to alert people of danger or tell the time.

**dooji**: [dudʒi] *n.*, Heroin. *Ifan yo go West Point yu can see de chiren dem smoking dooji.* (If you go West Point you can see the children them smoking dooji.) "If you go to West Point, you can see kids smoking heroin."

**door mouf**: [do mʌf] *n.*, Doorway. *Yu chiren muh na stan to de door mouf. Yu blocking de breeze.* (You children must not stand to the door mouth. You blocking the breeze.) "You children should not stand in the doorway. You are stopping the ventilation."

**dowry**: [da:ɹi] *n.*, Technically the "bride-price." In traditional marriages the prospective husband must provide a certain amount of goods and money to the bride's parents. After these payments are made the marriage is legally recognized by the community and government. *De man coming pay de woman dowry so dis marriage palava can fini.* (The man coming pay the woman dowry so this marriage palaver can finish.) "The man is going to pay the bride-price for the woman so the disagreement about the marriage can come to an end."

**dragon**: [dɹagɔ̃] *n.*, A malevolent reptilian spirit greatly feared in Liberia. Sometimes associated with the python. *Dragon fini swallow de baby, kwi medicine cyan do notting fo heen.* (Dragon finish swallow the baby. Kwi medicine can't do nothing for him.) "The dragon ate the baby's soul. Western medicine can't do anything for him."

**draw**: [dɹa] *v.*, To collect water. Used rather than "pump" or "fetch." *De lil geh coming draw wata fron de pump.* (The little girl coming draw water from the pump.) "The little girl is going to fetch some water from the hand-pump."

**dress**: [dɹɛs] 1. *v.*, To move over. *Yu can plea dress small?* (You can please dress small?) "Could you please move over?" 2. *v.*, To arrange attractively, decorate. *Dey fini dress de town fine fo de presiden coming.* (They finish dress the town fine for the president coming.) "They have made the town beautiful for the president's visit."

**dried dog**: [dɹaɪ dɔ] *idiom.*, Refers to a desirable, but ultimately unobtainable goal. A "catch-22" situation. For example, to start a business you need money, but you can't get loan from the bank because you have no capital. Comes from a common saying, "Dried dog sweet, but what we going to eat until the dog gets dried?" *During election tam da so so dried dog de politician dem can be promising.* (During election time that so so dried dog the politician them can be promising.) "Politicians make lots of promises they can't deliver at election time."

**drill**: [dɹɪl] *v.*, To march, as in a parade. A common school-related activity. *Dis coming Wenesday, we coming drill to Tubman High.* (This coming Wednesday we coming drill to Tubman High.) "Next Wednesday we're going to march at Tubman High."

**drip**: [dɹɪp] *n.*, An intravenous drip. Liberians generally believe injections and IVs to be more effective than pills. *Dis typhoid rally giving me har tam. A coming go to de clinic to tek drip.* (This typhoid really giving me hard time. I coming go to the clinic to take drip.) "This typhoid is really causing trouble for me. I am going to the clinic for an IV."

**drive**: [dɹaf] *v.*, To chase, to scare away. *Hoday A driving boid fron een my garden.* (Whole day I driving bird from in my garden.) "I am always chasing birds out of my garden."

**driver ans**: [dɹafa æs] *n.*, Blacks ants of the genus *Anomma* that form massive moving colonies. Can frequently be seen crossing roads and paths. The soldier ants have painful, but non-poisonous, bites. *Tek tam befo yu step een de driver ans.* (Take time before you step in the driver ants.) "Pay attention so you don't step in the driver ants."

**drop**: [dɹap] *v.*, 1. To get down, put down. *A wan drop to ELWA junshun.* (I want drop to ELWA junction.) "I want to get down at ELWA junction." 2. To fall down. *Wen de soyaman fiya heen, he drop skrate.* (When the soldier man fire him, he drop straight.) "When the soldier shot him, he fell down immediately."

**drunk**: [dɹɔ̃k] *v.*, To get someone drunk. *If A geh de contract A will tek yu to de bar an drunk yu.* (If I get the contract I will take you to the bar and drunk you.) "If I get the contract I will take you to the bar and get you drunk."

**druss**: [dɹʌs] "Drugs" *n.*, Western medicine. For traditional remedies see **medicine** and **country medicine**. *Dee druss dem wa A buy fron da black bagga cyan do no goo.* (These drugs them what I buy from that black bagger can't do no good.) "These drugs I brought from that quack don't do any good."

**dry**: [dɹaɪ] *adj.*, 1. Skinny, dehydrated, malnourished. *Dis baby looking too dry o!* (This baby looking too dry o!) "This baby looks very dehydrated!" 2. Without sauce (in reference to rice.) *Ma stomach giving me hard tam. A cyan mek ih wif torbagee na. Leh me jus eat small dry rice.* (My stomach giving me hard time. I can't make it with torbagee now. Let me just eat small dry rice.) "My stomach is hurting me. I'm not able to eat torbagee now. Let me just eat a little plain rice." 3. Impoverished, broke. *Ma man, tings too dry to de hus dee few days.* (My man, things too dry to the house these few days.) "My friend, things have been difficult at the house recently since the money ran out."

**dry coconut**: [dɹaɪ kokonə] *n.*, Fresh coconut in which the meat has ripened to the point of being firm and hard.

**dry fish**: [dɹaɪ fiʃ] *n.*, See **boney**

**dry meat**: [dɹaɪ mi] *n.*, See **bush meat**.

**dry monkey**: [dɹaɪ mɔ̃kɛ] *n.*, A common term for marasmus malnutrition. Children with this condition are very thin with a swollen belly.

**dry season**: [dɹaɪ sisɔ̃] *n.*, The period of dry weather between November and May. Cutting and burning of farms usually takes place in the driest months of December and January. *De ro fini spoil fron rainy season. Soon ah de dry season reesh ih coming start getting betta small small.* (The road finish spoil from rainy season. Soon as the dry season reach it coming start getting better small small.) "The roads have been ruined by the rainy season. As soon as the dry season is here they will start to improve." See also **rainy season**.

**du**: [du] *n.*, The Kusimanse Mongoose. *Crossarchus obscurus*. The most common mongoose in Liberia. Popular as pets. *De du da meat wa can kill snek fo common.* (The du that meat what can kill snake for common.) "Mongooses are the animals that commonly kill snakes."

**duap**: [dɔp] "daub" *v.*, To apply mud by hand to a framework of sticks. A traditional African method of building houses. *A coming daup my hus on Wenesday. You will be deh?* (I coming daub my house on Wednesday. You will be there?) "I am going to daub my house on Wednesday. Will you be there?"

**Dukor**: [dukɔ] *n.*, 1. Another name for the city of Monrovia, commonly used by tribes in the interior. Probably derived from the Mandingo *du ko*, "beyond the Du river." 2. The Du Court Hotel on Mamba Point in Monrovia. Once a luxurious tourist spot, it was ruined during the war.

**dumboy**: [dʌ̃mboɪ] *n.*, A thick cassava dough. Often served with clear spicy broth called **slippery sauce**. Eaten by forming the dough into balls, dipping in the sauce, and swallowing them whole. *Ma, yu rally know ha to fis dumboy de correc way!* (Ma, you really know how to fix dumboy the correct way!) "Mother, you really know the right way to prepare dumboy." See also **GB**.

**dumpile**: [dʌ̃mpaɪ] "dump pile" *n.*, A garbage pile or dump site. *Yu muh na chunk de dite on de ro. Yu muh chunk ih een de dumpile!* ("You must not chunk the dirt on the road. You must chunk it in the dumpile.) "You should not throw trash on the road. You should throw it away in the garbage pile."

**dusta**: [dʌsta] "duster" *n.*, Used rather than "eraser" for the tool used to clean a blackboard.

**dusty ro**: [dʌsti ɹo] "dusty road" *n.*, A dirt road. *Yu can be bouncing too mush on de dusty ro.* (You can be bouncing too much on the dusty road.) "You get bounced a lot on the dirt road."

**duwa**: [duwa] "dwarf" *n.*, Small, human-like creatures believed to inhabit the forests and mountains. Noted for their great strength and backwards-pointing feet. Greatly feared by many in Liberia. Sometimes associated with **jina**. *De hunta dem de one wa can be seeing de duwa.* (The hunter them the one what can be seeing the duwa.) "The hunters are the ones who can see dwarfs."

**dynamo**: [daɪnɛmo] *n.*, A generator. *Wa happing de dynamo cut so?* (What happening the dynamo cut so?) "Why did the generator cut off like that?"

# E

**easy**: [esi] *adj.*, Easygoing, amiable. *John say he can enjoy ha Martha way too easy so.* (John say he can enjoy how Martha way too easy so.) "John says he likes how Martha is so easygoing."

**eat**: [itˀ] *v.*, 1. To consume food. In Liberia it is considered very rude to eat in the presence of others without offering some of the food. See also **chop**. 2. To embezzle money. *Doh lawyer dem fini eating de money.* (The lawyer them finish eating the money.) "Those lawyers embezzled all the money." 3. To have sex. Slang. *Ifan yu na buy de ting for me, yu ain going eat tonight.* (If you not buy the thing for me, you ain't going eat tonight.) "If you don't buy this thing for me, I will not let you sleep with me tonight." 4. To capture an opponent's game pieces. *Ma king coming eat all yo seed.* (My king coming eat all your seed.) "My king is going to capture all your pieces." 5. To consume the soul of another person through witchcraft, causing imminent sickness and death. *De zoe fini kesh de witch wa eat my baby.* (The zoe finish catch the witch what eat my baby.) "The zoe has caught the witch who ate my baby's soul."

**eat ma eyeball**: [i ma abɔ] "eat my eyeball" *idiom.*, To rip someone off, to cheat. *Dis small punkin $200 L.D? Yu wan eat my eyeball?* (This small pumpkin $200 L.D.? You want eat my eyeball?) "This little pumpkin is $200 (LD)? Are you trying to rip me off?"

**eddo**: [ɛdo] *n.*, The coco-yam, taro. The edible tuber of the *Colocasia escalenta* or *Xanthosoma sagittifolium*. The large leaves resemble elephant ears. *De eddo to de garden coming on fine.* (The eddoes to the garden coming on fine.) "The eddoes in the garden are growing nicely."

**een de botto**: [ĩ dɛ batɔ] "in the bottle" *adj.*, To be drunk. Intoxicated. *Sam wa een de botto de tam he come home las night.* (Sam was in the bottle the time he come home last night.) Sam was drunk when he got home last night."

**eenfron**: [ĩfɹɔ̃] "in front" *adv.*, Forward, straight ahead. *A reeshing eenfron small.* (I reaching in front small.) "I am going ahead a little ways."

**eenside**: [ĩsaɪ] "inside" *prep.* 1. Used more commonly than simply "in." *Da papay eenside de hus.* (The papay is inside the house.) "The old man is in the house. 2. To be part of something. *A na eenside dis yo peepo society bisneh.* (I not inside this your people society business.) "I'm not a part of your people's secret society affairs."

**eh**: [é] *interj.*, An expression of surprise.

**elda**: [ɛda] "elder" *n.*, May be used as a title of respect for older men. In tribal settings elders represent their extended family group in official councils. *De town chief an de elda dem fini mek law say no one muh cut palm nut agin dis yeah.* (The town chief and the elders them finish make law say no one must cut palm nut again this year.) "The town chief and the elders have made a law that says nobody should cut anymore palm nuts this year."

**elk deer**: [ɛk diɛ] *n.*, The Bongo. *Tragelaphus euryceros.* The largest antelope species in Liberia. Has a red coat with white markings and prominent horns.

**embarrass**: [embaɹas] *v.*, To cause difficulty, to inconvenience. Used differently than Standard English (for this see **shame**.) *De elephan dem rally embarrassing we de farmer on dis side.* (The elephant them really embarrassing we the farmer on this side.) "Elephants are really creating problems for us farmers in this area."

**enjoy**: [ɛd͡ʒɔɪ] *v.*, To get all the benefit or pleasure out of a situation. Has a stronger meaning in Liberian English than Standard English. *A wa enjoying plenty een Monrovia.* (I was enjoying plenty in Monrovia.) "I was having the time of my life in Monrovia."

**enjoymen**: [ɛd͡ʒɔɪmɛ̃] "enjoyment" *n.*, Pleasure, usually in a carefree, illicit context. *Musu say Liberian man luf too mush enjoymen, da wa mek ih hard fo dem to succeed een bisneh.* (Musu said Liberian man love too much enjoyment. That what make it hard for them to succeed in business.) "Musu said Liberian men are only interested in having a good time. That's why it's hard for them to succeed in business ventures."

**enough**: [inʌf] *adj.*, Used differently than Standard English, meaning more than sufficient, a lot of something. *Dey geh enough potato greens to de markeh na.* (They get enough potato greens to the market now.) "They have a lot of potato greens in the market now."

**enta**: [ɛ̃ta] "enter" *v.*, Often used rather than "go inside." *Las night driver ans enta de hus an drive uh fron deh.* (Last night driver ants enter the house and drive us from there.) "Last night driver ants went inside our house and drove us from there."

**equal**: [ikua] *adj.*, Of the same level or social status. *Yu an mysef na equal!* (You and me not equal.) "You and I are not peers!"

**ewasince**: [ɛwasĩs] "ever since" *adv.*, Some time ago, already. *De pekin been having malaria ewasince.* (The pekin been having malaria ever since.) "The little boy has had malaria for a long time now."

**excuse**: [ɛksius] *interj* 1. Often used instead of "good-bye" to indicate one's parting. 2. A shortened form of "excuse me." Used when try to pass through a crowd or cut into line.

**eye turning:** [aɪ tʌɲĩ] *idiom.,* To be dizzy, drunk. *Afta Wuluba fini de cane juice hih eye wa turning.* (After Wuluba finish the cane juice his eyes were turning.) "When Wuluba was done drinking the cane liquor he was drunk."

# F

**fain**: [faĩ] "faint" *v.*, Used instead of pass out, go unconscious, knock out, etc. *De tam de man blow me, A fain skrate.* (The time the man blow me, I faint straight.) "When the man hit me, I immediately passed out."

**fall off**: [fal ɔf] *v.*, To fall apart, break apart. *Ma life jus falling off dee few days.* (My life just falling off these few days.) "My life is falling apart these days."

**false**: [fals] *adj.*, Imitation. For opposite of "true" see **lie**. *Da woman wearing false haih.* (That woman wearing false hair.) "That woman is wearing false hair."

**fanga**: [fãŋga] *n.*, A small, two-sided pressure drum. Held under the armpit. The player can change the pitch of the drum by applying pressure to the cords attached to the head, causing the drum to "talk" by mimicking the tones of a spoken language.

**fanner**: [fãna] 1. *n.*, A flat woven basket used to winnow rice. *De fanner una de keeshin.* (The fanner under the kitchen.) "The fanner is under the kitchen." 2. *v.*, To separate the chaff from the rice kernel with a rice fanner. *Wen she fini beating de rice she goin fanner ih.* (When she finish beating the rice she going fanner it.) "When she is done pounding the rice she will fan it."

**Fanti**: [fãti] *n.*, A Kwa speaking ethnic group originally from Ghana. Known for their mastery of the sea. Many make their living as fishermen, living in small settlements along the Liberian coast. *Fanti man newa see rotten fish.* (Fanti man never see rotten fish.) "A Fanti man has never seen a rotten fish (i.e. A Fanti man can always find a way to reprocess a fish and sell it)."

**Fanti cloth**: [fãti klɔ] *n.*, Brightly colored African cloth. Originally worn by the Fanti, but later popularized among other Liberian people. See also **lappa**.

**farina**: [faɹina] *n.*, Dried cassava flakes. Often served with sugar and powdered milk for breakfast. *Wen A fini harvesing my cassava, A coming mek ih wif farina.* (When I finish harvesting my cassava, I coming make it with farina.) "After I harvest my cassava, I will make it into farina."

**farm**: [fã:m] *n.*, Land used for agricultural purposes. Most farms in Liberia are cultivated through slash and burn agricultural. Most have small shelters called kitchens (see **kishen**) where harvested crops are stored and cooking takes place. Some people build small houses for sleeping on their farm during labor intensive seasons. Interestingly, Liberians refer to rice and rubber plantations as "farms," while cocoa, coffee, cassava, and vegetable patches are called "gardens." *A coming brush my farm dis week.* (I coming brush my farm this week.) "I am going to clear my farm this week."

**farm ro**: [fã:m ɹo] "farm road" *n.*, A path leading through the forest to a farm. *A kill one ans bear on my farm ro today.* (I kill one ants bear on my farm road today.) "I killed a pangolin on the path to my farm today."

**farm ro far**: [fã:m ɹo fa] "farm road far" *idiom.*, To be deaf, hard of hearing. *Don mine da ole ma. Hur farm ro far.* (Don't mind that old ma. Her farm road far.) "Never mind that old lady. She is hard of hearing."

**fat**: [fæt˥] *adj.*, A healthy plumpness of body. Highly valued in Liberian culture. As opposed to **dry**. *Eh my man. Yu looking too fat na!* (Hey, my man. You looking too fat now!) "Hey buddy, you're looking nice and plump now!"

**fearfo**: [fijafo] "fearful" *adj.*, Dangerous, scary, causing trepidation. *Lepor da fearfo animo. Wen yu budduh wif heen een de bush yo heart can cut skrate.* (Leopard that fearful animal. When you butt up with him in the bush your heart can cut straight.) "The leopard is a scary animal. If you run into him in the forest your heart skips a beat." See also **scary**.

**feeling** [filĩ] *n.*, Compassion, pity. *De tam A see da man sitting lonely so, A geh feeling fo heen.* (The time I see the man sitting lonely so, I get feeling for him.) "When I saw that man sitting all alone, I felt sorry for him."

**fever grass**: [fivɔ gɹas] *n.*, Lemon grass. *Cymbopogon spp.* Commonly used for medicinal teas.

**fever leaf**: [fiva lif] *n.*, The wild basil plant. *Ocimum gratissimum.* Used for a sauce served over rice. Also has medicinal value.

**fever tea**: [fivɔ ti] *n.*, A herbal tea made from lemon grass.

**fierce**: [fiɛs] *adj.*, Good looking, handsome. *Da boy too fierce.* (That boy too fierce.) "That boy is very handsome."

**fekefeke**: [fɛkɛfɛkɛ] *adj.*, Insignificant, worthless, etc. *Ma sassywoo da na fekafeka one.* (My sassywood that not fekafeka one.) "My sassywood is not worthless." i.e. "My sassywood is very powerful."

**fine**: [fãj] 1. *adj.*, Beautiful, attractive. *Fine geh, come yah.* (Fine girl, come here.) "Pretty girl, come here." 2 *adv.*, Very much so, in a positive sense (unlike the American usage "adequate.") *She can cook ih fine.* (She can cook it fine.) "She can cook that dish very well." See also **ba way**. 3. *interj.*, Exactly so, an exclamation of agreement or satisfaction. *Fine! Da de ting A been toking.* (Fine! That the thing I been talking.) "Exactly so! That's what I was talking about."

**fini**: [fɪni] "finish" 1. Completive aspect marker. *She fini go to de markeh.* (She finish go to the market.) "She went to the market." 2. *v.*, Depleted, run out. *De sauce fini. You wan so A muh eat dry rice?* (The sauce finish. You want so I must eat dry rice?) "The sauce is gone. Do you want me to eat plain rice?" 3. *adj.*, To be worn out, used. *De car tiya fini.* (The car tire finish.) "The car's tires are worn out." 4. *adj.*, Completely, totally, thoroughly. *Da woman fini ugly.* (That woman finish ugly.) "That woman is incredibly ugly."

**fis**: [fɪs] "fix" *v.*, 1. To repair. *Yu can fis cycle?* (You can fix cycle?) "Do you know how to repair bicycles?" 2. To build, build, prepare. *Da man can fis bamboo beh.* (That man can fix bamboo bed.) "That man knows how make rattan beds."

**fish basket**: [fɪʃ bæskɛ] *n.*, A small fish trap woven from raffia. *A collec plenty crawfish een my fish basket dis morning.* (I collect plenty crawfish in my fish basket this morning.) "I gathered a lot of prawns in my fish basket this morning."

**fish cup**: [fɪʃ kʌ] *n.*, A tin of cooked fish such as mackerel or salmon canned in tomato juice or oil. Commonly available throughout Liberia. See also **tinapaw**.

**fishing**: [fɪʃi] *v.*, To fish. *A coming fishing to Lofa riva.* (I coming fishing to Lofa river.) "I'm going to go fishing in the Lofa river."

**fiya**: [faja] "fire" *v.*, To shoot at. *A wa coming fiya de red deer, buh my gunshot fini.* (I was coming fire the red deer, but my gunshot finish.) "I was going to shoot the red deer, but my shots had run out." Not used to mean dismissal from one's place of employment. For this, see **sack**.

**fiya behine**: [faja bihaï] "fire behind" *idiom.*, To apply pressure in order to force a person to do something. *Da man na wan fini dis contrac, so A coming puh fiya behine heen.* (The man not want finish this contract, so I coming put fire behind him.) "That man doesn't want to finish his contract, so I'm going to put pressure on him."

**Firestone**: [fajastõ] *n.*, The Firestone rubber company. Operates a large rubber plantation and processing plant in Harbel near Robertsfield.

**flash**: [flaʃ] *v.*, 1. To splash. *De tam ih raining, taxi driva quick to flash peepo.* (The time it raining, taxi driver quick to flash people.) "When it's raining, taxi drivers often splash pedestrians." 2. To call someone's cell phone, but hang up before the person answers. Since cell phone companies in Liberia only charge the caller and not the recipient, a person may do this so the expense of the call will be on the person with whom he wishes to talk. See **beep**. 3. To take a photograph. *Wa happing yu jus flash people? Yu muh aks me befo yu tek my pisha!* (What happen you just flash people? You must ask me before you take my picture.) "Why do you just take pictures of people? You should ask me before you take my picture!"

**flat mouf:** [fla mof] "flat mouth" *adj.,* Used in reference to people with small lips, such as Caucasians.

**flok:** [flɔk˺] "flog" *v.,* To beat. *Move fron on de ro befo A flok yu!* (Move from on the road before I flog you!") "Get out of the road or I will beat you!"

**fo common:** [fo kamɔ̃] "for common" *adv.,* Commonly, often, without difficulty. *My fren een Tappita can kill bush cow fo common.* (My friend in Tappita can kill bush cow for common.) "My friend in Tappita kills forest buffalo like it is nothing."

**fo long:** [fo lɔ̃] "for long" *adv.,* An abbreviation of "for a long time." *Fo long A been suffring from back complain.* (For long I been suffering from back complaint.) "I've been having back problems for a long time."

**foni:** [foni] *n.,* A type of grain most commonly known in English as sorgum. From the Mandingo language. See **hungry rice.**

**fo notting:** [fo nʌfi] "for nothing" *adj.,* Worthless. An abbreviated form of "good for nothing." *My fren fo notting cabmoto fini heesh een de pata-pata.* (My friend for nothing cab-moto finish hitch in the patapata.) "My friend's good for nothing truck got stuck in the mud."

**fooly:** [fuli] "foolish" *adj.* Stupid, incompetent. Considered a grave insult in Liberia. *Dis yo fooly man yah fini eat all de money.* (This your foolish man here finish eat all the money.) "Your stupid friend here has spent all the money on himself."

**fooly tongor:** [fuli tãgɔ] *n.,* The Gray Duiker. *Cephalophus maxwelli liberiensis.* A small gray-brown antelope, about 14 inches high, with small horns. A common bushmeat. *A kesh one fooly tongor een my trap las ni.* (I catch one fooly tongor in my trap last night.) "I caught a gray duiker in my snare last night."

**foot:** [fʊt˺] *n.,* Used in a more general sense in Liberia to refer to the entire leg. *De tam de cassava snek boin George, hih ho foot swell uh.* (The time the cassava snake burn George, his whole foot swell up.) "When the Gabon viper bit George, his whole leg swelled up."

**football:** [fʊbɔ] *n.,* 1. The game of soccer. *We going on de fiel to play football.* (We going on the field to play football.) "We are going on the field to play football." 2. A soccer ball.

**fo tru:** [fo tɹu] "for true" *adv.,* Truly, really. *Fo tru, de ole ma die o.* (For true, the old ma die o.) "The old lady really died."

**fox**: [fas] n., The slender mongoose. *Galerella sanguinea.* Similar in appearance to a weasel with a reddish coat and a black-tipped tail. Very common in the brush around towns and villages. True foxes are unknown in Liberia. *De fox grap one oh my chicken dis gone Friday.* (The fox grab one of my chicken this gone Friday.) "A slender mongoose caught one of my chickens this past Friday."

**free**: [fɹi] v., Used rather than "release." *Wen de judge cut de case, dey free de man.* (When the judge cut the case, they free the man.) "When the judge gave the verdict on the case, they released the man."

**freen show**: [fɹĩ ʃo] "film show" n., A movie, video, film. *Me pa, A ain love da ola freen show.* (My part, I ain't love that other film show.) "As for me, I don't like that other movie." See also **African show**.

**fren**: [fɹẽ] "friend" n., Fellow, another of the same kind. *Ha yu peepo can be causing palava wif yo fren Christian dem?* (Why you people can be causing palaver with your friend Christian them?) Why do you people pick fights with your fellow Christians?"

**fresh co**: [fɹɛʃ ko] "fresh cold" n., The common cold, a runny nose. A common problem for village children. *Ma peepo, dis fresh co bisneh rally giving uh hard tam.* (My people, this fresh cold business really giving us hard time.) "Friends, all these colds are really causing problems for us."

**frisky**: [fɹɪski] adj., Energetic, active, often with the sense of being troublesome or naughty. Usually said of children. *Hoday da frisky pekin can gii hih ma hard tam.* (Whole day that frisky pekin can give his ma hard time.) "That naughty little boy always gives his mother trouble."

**frog baby**: [fɹa bebi] n., A tadpole. Aquatic frog larva. *De frog baby plenty een de wata.* (The frog baby plenty in the water.) "There are a lot of tadpoles in the water."

**fukuh**: [fʌkʌ] "fuck up" v., To ruin, spoil. This word is commonly heard in Liberia without the vulgar sense it carries in Standard English. *Nail fukuh my motobike tiya.* (Nail fuck up my motorbike tire.) "A nail messed up my motorbike's tire."

**fuel oil**: [fiu ɔj] n., Diesel fuel. *A wan buy some fuel oil fo my cabmoto.* (I want buy some fuel oil for my cab-moto.) "I want some diesel fuel for my truck."

**fufu**: [fufu] n., Fermented cassava dough. A staple food of southeastern Liberia. Dipped in an oily sauce and swallowed in small chunks. *A ain love fufu rotten sen.* (I ain't love fufu rotten scent.) "I don't like fufu's fermented smell."

**Fula**: [fula] *n.,* The Fulani ethnic group. Originally from Guinea and Sierra Leone, many work in Liberia as merchants and shopkeepers. They are known for their good business skills and devotion to the Islamic religion.

**fulluh**: [folʌ] "full up." *adj.,* Very full. *Her gallon fulluh wif reh oil.* (Her gallon full up with red oil.) "Her container is full of red oil."

**fun**: [fʌ̃] *n.,* A joke. *He tok one fun wa mek me laugh plenty.* (He told one fun what make me laugh plenty.) "He told a joke that made me laugh a lot."

**fusu**: [fusu] *adv.,* Nothing, anything. *Afta Flomo tok de ole man cun say fusu.* (After Flomo talk the old man couldn't say fusu.) "After Flomo talked the old man couldn't say anything."

**fut**: [fʊt˺] *adj.,* 1. Full, flooded, filled to the point of overflowing. *Dis riva fut fron rainy season.* (This river full from rainy season.) "This river is flooded from rainy season." 2. Ripe. *De golden plum ain fut yeh.* (The golden plum ain't full yet.) "The golden plums aren't ripe yet."

# G

**gallon**: [galõ] *n.*, A plastic container used to store liquid, usually with a screw-on lid. *Bring me de gallon so A can go draw wata.* (Bring me the gallon so I can go draw water.) "Bring me the container so I can go get some water."

**gambo seed**: [gæmbɔ si] "gamble seed" *n.*, Money cowry. A small white sea shell formally used as currency in West Africa. Valued now in traditional gift exchanges and sacrifices. Also used by **molimen** to divine the future.

**ganja**: [gãd͡ʒa] *n.*, Marijuana. *Doh boys can be smoking plenty ganja een de ghetto.* (Those boys can be smoking plenty ganja in the ghetto.) "Those boys smoke a lot of dope in the drug house."

**gap**: [gæp] *adj.*, To be hungry. Slang. *Woman, A gapping ba way o!* (Woman, I gapping bad way o!) "Wife, I'm very hungry!"

**gape**: [gep] *v.*, To yawn. *De way yu gaping so, A hope yu na coming sleep.* (The way you gaping so, I hope you not coming sleep.) "With the way you are yawning, I hope you are not about to go to sleep."

**garage**: [gaɹaʒ] *n.*, Only used for a car repair shop.

**garee**: [gaɹi] *n.*, Dried cassava flakes mixed with sugar. Eaten as a breakfast food or snack.

**gate**: [get˺] *n.*, A checkpoint. *Een de war dey wa keshing peepo to de gate ouhside Gbarnga an killing dem fo common.* (In the war they was catching people to the gate outside Gbarnga and killing them for common.) "During the war they were catching people at the checkpoint outside of Gbarnga and killing them like it was nothing."

**GB**: [d͡ʒibi] *n.*, A cassava dough formed by boiling cassava and beating it in a mortar. Eaten by hand by pulling off pieces from the lump and dipping them into a spicy soup before swallowing. Allegedly an acronym for "Gio Bread." *Wen yu eat GB, yu muh na chew ih. Yu muh swallow ih skrate.* (When you eat GB, you must not chew it. You must swallow it straight.) "When you eat GB you should not chew it. You should swallow it right away." See also **dumboy**.

**gbala**: [g͡bala] *n.*, A general term for a weapon, including guns and knives. *Wen he see de rebo coming, he tek hih gbala an fiya dem skrate.* (When he see the rebels coming, he take hih gbala and fire them straight.) "When he saw the rebels coming, he took his weapon and shot at them immediately."

**gbalen**: [g͡balɛ̃] *n.*, Traditional cloth made from raffia fiber.

**gbana**: [g͡bana] *adj.*, Mischievous, rascally, unruly. *Dis yo son da real gbana pekin da.* (This your son that real gbana pekin that.) "Your son is a very unruly child." See also **frisky**.

**gbapleh**: [g͡baplɛ] *n.*, 1. A small finger-sized saltwater fish. Cheap and easily available. Considered somewhat of a poor man's food. Often used in making pepper soup. 2. A passive man who lacks the self-confidence to adapt to new situations and thus must be be "seasoned" by his wife to make him useful. Slang.

**gbassa jamba**: [g͡basa d͡ʒamb] *n.*, A common name for **cassava leaf** sauce. Borrowed from the Vai language. The Vai are known in Liberia for their love of this sauce.

**gbagon**: [g͡bagõ] *n.*, The rhinoceros beetle. *Oryctes spp.* A very large species of beetle which is attracted to artificial lights at night. Males have a prominent horn on their snout. Considered by some to be a delicacy.

**gbegbe**: [g͡beg͡be] *adj.*, Clear, straightforward, without deceit. Possibly from the Mandingo *gbe* "white, clear." The opposite of **katakata**. *Ah las Peye wa toking gbegbe.* (At last Peye was talking gbegbe.) "At last Peye was speaking the clear truth."

**gbelegbele**: [g͡bɛlɛg͡bɛlɛ] *adv.*, To take one's time, go nice and easy. *Ain yu see de way John coming gbelegbele?* (Ain't you see the way John coming gbelegbele?) "Don't you see how John is taking his time coming?"

**gbema**: [gbema] *n.*, Traditional music set to a fast-paced electronic beat. Usually sung in local languages.

**Gbi**: [g͡bi] *n.*, A small ethnic group (approximately 6,000) which resides in southern Nimba County. They speak a Kwa language related to Bassa. Since they were very isolated until recent decades, the Gbi are often overlooked in tribal listings.

**gbingbing**: [g͡big͡bĩ] *n.*, A large two headed drum. Played with a stick and hands.

**gboye**: [g͡bo je] "Boiled egg" *n.*, Hard boiled eggs. Often shouted by street venders.

**geh**: [gɛ] "get" *v.*, Used rather than "has" and "have." *A ain geh som.* (I ain't get some.) "I don't have any."

**geh bes**: [gɛ bɛs] "get best" *v.*, To win in the end, to be vindicated. *Da man tink he can insul me so? He shu know A going geh bes!* (The man think he can insult me so? He should know I going get best!) "If that guy thinks he can get away with insulting me like that, he should know I'm going to win in the end!"

**gehdah**: [gɛda] *n.,* 1. Gossip, salacious rumors. *Bindu been toking gehdah behine me say A an de bossman loving.* (Bindu been talking gehdah behind me say I and the bossman loving.) "Bindu has been spreading gossip behind my back saying that I am sleeping with the boss." 2. A person who spreads gossip. See also **besse** and **chechepolay.**

**geh mouf**: [mauf] "get mouth" *idiom.,* Used to describe people who talk too much, especially those prone to saying inappropriate things. *Da pekin geh mouf fo true.* (That pekin get mouth for true.) "That kid really talks too much."

**geh tam**: [gɛ tam] "get time" *v.,* Used rather than "to care." *Da man ain geh tam fo dis yo woman palava.* (That man ain't get time for this your woman palaver.) "That man doesn't care about your woman troubles."

**German plum**: [d͡ʒɛɹmɛ̃ plʌ̃] *n.,* A large, especially tasty, variety of mango. *Da crakay pekin break ih arm de tam he wa picking German plum.* (That crack head pekin break his arm the time he was picking German plum.) "That stubborn little boy broke his arm when he was picking mangoes."

**ghetto**: [gɛto] *n.,* A house used to do drugs. *Hoday doh grenna boys dem can be to de ghetto.* (Whole day those grenna boys them can be to the ghetto.) "Those gangsters are always hanging out in the drug house."

**Gio**: [gio] *n.,* More properly know as the *Dan*, this people group extents from eastern Liberia into Cote d'Ivoire. They speak a language in the south-east Mande group, and are closely related linguistically and culturally to the Mano. Primarily animistic with some Muslim and Christian presence.

**girlfriend/boyfriend**: [gɛfɹɛ̃] *n.,* A romantic partner. In Liberia these terms almost always imply a sexual relationship. For non-sexual romantic relationships it is better to call someone your "good friend" or simply say you are "dating."

**glass botto**: [glas bato] "glass bottle" *n.,* Often refers to shards of broken glass used to line the tops of cement walls for security purposes.

**gobachop**: [gobat͡ʃap] 1. *n.,* A market in the Red Light area of Monrovia. Literally, "go buy chop (food)." *A going Gobuychop to go look fo some fertilizer.* (I going Gobuychop to go look for some fertilizer.) "I'm going to Gobuychop to look for some fertilizer." 2. *adj.,* Selling goods at inflated prices. Justified by the phrase, *Yu chop, A chop.* "You chop, I chop" meaning, "We both make a profit." *Ma man, A ain lek yo gobuychop bisneh."* (My man, I ain't like your gobuychop business.) "Buddy, I don't like the way you manipulate your prices."

**gobachop official**: [gobat͡ʃap ofɪʃo] *n.,* A corrupt government worker. *Why A shu pay my taxes wen de gobachop official dem can just be eat-*

*ing de money?* (Why I should pay my taxes when the gobachop official them can just be eating the money.) "Why should I pay my taxes when corrupt government workers are simply embezzling the money?"

**go com**: [go kʌ̃] *v.,* To leave with the intent to return. *A go com.* (I go come.) "I'm leaving, but I'll be back."

**gohfada**: [gɔfada] "godfather" *n.,* A "sugar daddy." An older man who uses a younger girl for sex in exchange for money or goods. *Dey say Harriet geh gohfada wa can be giving her doh fine fine clo dem.* (They say Harriet got godfather what can be giving her those fine fine clothes them.) "They say Harriet has a sugar daddy who gives her those beautiful clothes."

**gohma**: [gɔma] "godma" *n.,* An older woman who uses a younger man for sex.

**Gola**: [gola] *n.,* An Atlantic-speaking ethnic group of western Liberia. Numbers approximately 110,000. Primarily animistic or Muslim, with some Christian presence. Gola is said to be one of the most difficult language in Liberia to learn.

**golden plum**: [godẽ plʌ̃] *n.,* The Ambarella. *Spondias cytherea.* A yellow, mango-like fruit popular in Liberia. *Golden plum sweet, buh dey ain fut yeh.* (Golden plum sweet, but they ain't full yet.) "Golden plums are tasty, but they are not yet ripe."

**gone**: [gɔ̃] *adj.* Past, in reference to days of the week. *Dih gone Friday A wen Kakata to buy slippa.* (This gone Friday I went Kakata to buy slipper.) "This past Friday I went to Kakata to buy flip-flops."

**goo**: [gu] "good." *adv.,* Used to mean "well." Often redoubled for emphasis. *He ain know ih goo goo.* (He ain't know it good good.) "He doesn't know it very well."

**gorilla**: [gɔɹla] *n.,* There are no true gorillas in Liberia, but this term is occasionally heard in reference to old, very large chimpanzees. See also **baboon**.

**gown**: [gaũ] *v.,* To dress someone in a chief's gown as a sign of honor and appreciation. Often done at graduation programs or other important occasions. *Ah de program we gown de bossman.* (At the program we gown the bossman.) "We dressed our boss in a gown at the program."

**grass**: [gɹæs] *n.,* Weeds, unwanted plants. *A sen de pekin to go rudduh de grass fron de garden.* (I sent the pekin to go root up the grass from the garden.) "I sent the boy to go uproot the weeds from the garden."

**grasscutta**: [gɹaskuta] "grasscutter" *n.* The Cane Rat. *Thryonomys swinderianus swinderianus.* Also called **ground hog**. A large brown rodent, considered a major pest in village farms. *De grasscutta fini spoil all my rice.* (The grass cutter finish spoil all my rice.) "The cane rats ruined all my rice."

**gravy**: [gɹavi] *n.,* An oily sauce made without greens. Served over rice. *De woman tek de tomato wif de chicken soup and mek if wif chicken gravy.* (The woman take the tomato with the chicken soup and make it with chicken gravy.) "The woman took the tomatoes and bullion cubes and made them into chicken gravy sauce." See also **soup**.

**greasy**: [gɹisi] *adj.,* Oily, shiny. Often said of a person's hair in a positive sense. *Hur hair looking too fine an greasy.* (Her hair looking too fine and greasy.) "Her hair looks beautiful and shiny."

**Grebo**: [gɹebo] *n.,* A cluster of related people group in south-eastern Liberia who speak Kwa languages. Total population is approximately 265,000. They were lumped together in the late 20th century by the Liberian government for political expediency. Christian and traditional African religionists.

**greegree**: [gɹigɹi] *n.,* An old term from West African Pidgin English meaning charms or amulets. In Liberia these are more commonly referred to as **medicine**.

**green monkey**: [gɹĩ mɔ̃kɛ] *n.,* The Callithrix monkey. *Chlorocebus sabaeus.* A small species that has a tan colored coat with a slightly green hue.

**greens**: [gɹĩs] *n.,* Any leafy vegetable. Often cooked with oil for "rice and soup" (e.g. cassava leaf, potato greens, etc.)

**greet**: [gɹit'] *v.,* In Liberia greetings are very important. It is considered extremely rude to pass through someone's yard without greeting him or her. *Wa happing yu cyan greet peepo?* (What happening you can't greet people?) "Why don't you greet people?"

**grip**: [gɹɪp] *n.,* Used rather than "suitcase." *A see one fine grip to de markeh, buh A ain know ha A going buy ih.* (I see one fine grip to the market, but I ain't know how I going buy it.) "I saw a nice suitcase in the market, but I don't know how I will buy it."

**gripper**: [gɹɪpɔ] *n.,* "grouper" Refers to varies ocean fish in the family Serranidae. Characterized by a large mouth. Some species can grow very large. Considered a delicacy.

**grumbo**: [gɹombo] *n.,* See **halahala**.

**grumbo pekin**: [gɹombo pikĩ] *n.,* A person who likes to stir up trouble.

**gronna**: [gɹonʌ] *adj.*, Rebellious, disrespectful, sexually promiscuous. *A ain know wa mek ih she jus can be acting da gronna way.* (I ain't know what make it she just can be acting that gronna way.) "I don't know why she always running wild."

**gronna boy**: [gɹonʌ bɔɪ] *n.*, A juvenile delinquent, gangster. *Doh gronna boys dem too mush to Red Light."* (Those gronna boys them too much to Red Light.) "There are a lot of gangsters around the Red Light area."

**ground hog**: [gɹaũ hɔ] *n.*, See **grasscutta**.

**groundpea**: [gɹaũmpi] *n.*, Used rather than "peanut." *A plan groundpea wif okra to my garden.* (I plant ground pea with okra to my garden.) "I planted peanuts and okra in my garden."

**guh**: [gʌ] "gut" *n.*, Stomach. *Ma guh geh complain.* (My gut get complaint.) "I have a stomach problem." See also **belly**.

**guinea fowl**: [gɪni fau] *n.*, A chicken-sized domesticated bird. *Numida meleagris.* Since guinea fowl hens are poor mothers, their eggs are often given to chickens to be hatched and raised. Several wild species also live in Liberia. Has a loud, harsh call.

**gun-proof**: [gʌ̃pɹuf] *adj.*, See **bulleh proof**.

**gunshot**: [gʌ̃ʃat'] *n.*, Used more commonly than "bullet."

**gutta**: [guətə] *n,*. Used more often than "ditch." *Haccome de donfa dem can alway be een de gutta?* (How come donfa them can always be in the gutter?) "Why are ducks always in the ditches?"

**gwana**: [guana] "iguana" *n.*, The Nile Monitor lizard. *Varanus nilotictus.* A large black lizard with yellow spots. Often lives near rivers. Has a powerful bite and can use its tail as a whip.

# H

**haccome**: [hakʌ̃] "how come" adv. Often used in place of "why." *Da haccome A reesh Monrovia soon.* (That how come I reach Monrovia soon.) "That's why I arrived in Monrovia early." See **wa happing**.

**hard heh**: [ha: hɛ] "hard-head" *adj.* Stubborn, insolent, rebellious. *Dis lil geh yah too hard heh. De ting A say she muh do, she refuse.* (This little girl here too hard head. The think I say she must do, she refuse.) "This little girl is very stubborn. She refuses to do the things I tell her to do." See also **crakay**.

**hard tam**: [ha: tam] "hard time" *n.*, Difficulties, troubles *A been keshing too mush of hard tam fron dis malaria bisneh.* (I been catching too mush oh hard time from this malaria business.) "Malaria has been giving me a lot of trouble."

**hard to**: [ha: tu] "hard to" *adv.*, Difficult, tedious. *Bush cow hard to done.* (Bush cow hard to done.) "Bush cow meat takes a long time to cook."

**hala**: [hala] "holler" *v.*, Used rather than yell, shout, scream, etc. *De tam Momo see de heart man to de junshun, he start to hala ba way.* (The time Momo see the heart man to the junction, he start to holler bad way.) "When Momo saw the heart man at the intersection, he started screaming loudly."

**halahala**: [halahala] "holler holler" *n.*, 1. Excessive shouting, *Stop da halahala na!* (Stop the holler holler now!) "Shop all that shouting now!" 2. A large dispute or argument.

**half dry** : [akɹa grʌ̃ pi] *adj.*, Fish or bush-meat that has been smoked to a rubbery consistency. Usually soaked in water before being cooked. *Ma pa love to eat da half dry boney.* (My pa love to eat that half dried boney.) "My dad loves to eat that half-dried herring."

**half-way**: [hæf we] *adv.*, In Liberian culture it is considered polite to accompany one's guests a certain distance on the road. *When Augustus fini eating, A carry heen half-way.* (When Augustus finish eating, I carry him half-way.) "When Augustus was done eating, I accompanied him half-way (to his house)."

**han**: [hæ̃] "hand" *n.*, 1. Used in a broader sense to refer to any part of one's arm from the shoulder to the hand. *Ma han haiting me.* (My hand hurting me.) "My arm is hurting me." 2. Figurative for ability to provide. *A na geh han to fee dee chiren.* (I not get hand to feed these children.) "I don't have means to provide for these kids." 3. Figurative for involvement in something. *A ain geh han eenside dis krokoji bisneh.* (I can't get hand inside this krokogee business.) "I don't have any part of this crooked dealing."

**han fall don**: [hæ fɔ dã] "hand fall down" *idiom.*, To have a loss, a setback. *A wa hoping to mek plenty money buh my han fall don een dis bisneh.* (I was hoping to make plenty money but my hand fall down in this business.) "I was hoping to make a lot of money, but I suffered a setback"

**hang heh**: [hã hɛ] "hang heads" *v.*, To meet together in private, to consult over an important matter. *De men dem coming hang heh.* (The men them coming hang head.) "The men are going to have a meeting."

**hard**: [ha:] *adv.*, To happen with difficulty. *Wata hard to dry een dis riwa.* (Water hard to dry in this river.) "It is very rare for this river to run dry."

**harmattan**: [hamatã] *n.*, A yearly occurrence in which dry winds from the Sahara carry dust throughout West Africa. In Liberia, this usually occurs at the end of December. While the whole country is affected, its effects are most noted in northern Liberia where the harmattan coats everything in dust, causes impressive sunset and makes the night temperatures relatively cool.

**harmattan lily**: [hamatã lɪli] *n.*, A species of Amaryllis lily common throughout Liberia. Blooms during the dry season with dusty orange, trumpet-shaped flowers at the head of a long stalk.

**hatayee**: [hataji] *n.*, A strong drink made from black "gunpowder" tea. From the Arabic word *chai* "tea." Especially popular with the Mandingo and Fula people. It is brewed in small pots over coal. After the tea is poured, more water and sugar is added to the pot, making each successive round less bitter and sweeter than the last. *Wif hatayee, da round tdee wa can be sweet.* (With hatayee, that round three what can be sweet.) "With hatayee, round three is the one that is especially delicious. "

**haul**: [hɔ] *v.*, 1. To pull. *Da doh Kru boy dem wa wa hauling deh nets on shore.* (That those Kru boy them what was hauling their nets on shore.) "It was those Kru boys who were pulling their nets on shore." 2. To carry. *A wan use my cab-moto to haul da crush rock.* (I want use my cab-moto to haul that crush rock.) "I want to use my truck to carry that crushed rock."

**have seat**: [haf sit'] *v.*, Used rather than sit down, be seated. *Yor can have seat.* (You can have seat.) "You all can be seated."

**heart bitta**: [ha: bɪta] "heart bitter" *adv.*, To be angry. *Hih heart bitta becau hih fren mean heen.* (His heart bitter because his friend mean him.) "He is angry because his friend snubbed him."

**heart boining**: [ha: boĩnĩ] "heart burning" *v.,* Deep emotional hurt, sadness. *Ma heart boining fo de ole ma wa jus die.* (My heart burning for the old ma what just die.) "I am very sad about the old lady who just died."

**heart clean**: [ha: klĩ] *adj.,* To be honest, with good intentions, to have integrity. *Ma Musu heart clean. She won do susha ting.* (Ma Musu heart clean. She wouldn't do such a thing.) "Ma Musu is honest. She wouldn't do such a thing."

**heart cut**: [ha: kʌt'] *v.,* For one's heart to skip a beat, to be scared. *Wen A see de snek to de door mouf ma heart cut.* (When I see the snake to the door mouth my heart cut.) "When I saw the snake in the doorway my heart skipped a beat."

**heart fall don**: [ha: fɔ dã] "heart fall down" *v.,* To be saddened or discouraged. *De tam de fwiting start een Monrovia, ma heart fall don.* (The time the fighting start in Monrovia, my heart fall down.) "When the fighting started in Monrovia, I was grieved."

**heart lay don**: [ha: le dã] "heart lay down" *adv.,* To be deeply contented or satisfied. *Wen A see da lil geh fine hur ma, ma heart will lay don.* (When I see the little girl find her ma, my heart will lay down.) "I will be very happy when I see that little girl find her mother."

**heart man**: [ha: mɛ̃] *n.,* A hit man hired to procure human body parts for ritual sacrifices. Aspiring politicians and others in secret societies are believed to commission such sacrifices in an attempt to procure occultic power for themselves. *Yu chiren muh tek tam walking on da ro befo de heart man kesh yu.* (You children must take time walking on the road before the heart man catch you.) "You children need to be careful walking on that road so the heart man doesn't catch you."

**heart sii don**: [ha: sɪ dã] "heart sit down" *v.,* See **heart lay don.**

**heateh**: [hitɛ] "heated" *adj.,* To be hot. Liberians describe the state of being overheated with this word, rather than "hot." *A too heateh.* (I too heated.) "I'm really hot."

**heavy**: [hɛvi] *adv.,* 1. Great. *De motobike wa running wif heavy speed.* (The motorbike was running with heavy speed.) "The motorbike was going very fast." 2. Strong, significant. *One heavy breeze knock da tree down.* (One heavy breeze knock the tree down.) "A strong wind knocked that tree down."

**heesh**: [hiʃ] "hitch" *v.,* Used rather than stick, catch, adhere. *A wa coming tok ih, buh ma tongue heesh.* (I was coming talk it, but my tongue hitch.) "I was going to say it, but I couldn't bring myself to talk."

**heh tie**: [hɛ taɪ] "head-tie" *n.,* A scarf or piece of cloth worn decoratively on the head by women.

**heh wife**: [hɛ taɪ] "head wife" *n.,* This term refers to the wife who is appointed by the husband to manage his other wives and oversee household matters.

**hellava**: [hɛləvə] "hell of a" *adj.,* Big, strong, impressive. Not considered profane in Liberian English. *Deh one hellava palava going on een town na.* (There one hell of a palaver going on in town now.) "There is a huge argument going on in town now."

**herbalist**: [ɛɹbalis] *n.,* A person who uses natural remedies to heal. This term is used by more educated Liberians in reference to those who practice **country medicine**.

**hero**: [hiɹo] *n.,* 1. Champion, expert. May be used ironically. *He de hero fo eating.* (He the hero for eating.) "He's the champion eater." 2. The protagonist in a film. *Da guy cyan die. He de hero.* (That guy can't die. He the hero.) "That guy won't die. He's the good guy."

**hinterland**: [hĩtʌlæ̃] *n.,* An antiquated term for the interior regions of Liberia, in contrast to the coastal, "civilized," areas. See **interior** and **upcountry**.

**hipco**: [hɪpko] *n.,* 1. Locally produced hip-hop and rap music which uses "colloquial" Liberian English. 2. The dress, dance and subculture associated with hipco music.

**Hitler War**: [hĩtla wɔ] "Hitler's War" *n.,* Refers to World War II (1939-1945.) In contrast, *World War Two* in common Liberian parlance refers to the second phase of the final siege of Monrovia.

**hobojoe**: [hobod͡ʒo] *n.,* A prostitute, loose woman. Slang usage.

**hoday**: [hode] "whole day" *adv.,* 1. All the time. *Hoday doh chiren dem can be making palava.* (Whole day those children them can be making palaver.) "Those kids are always fighting." 2. Literally "all day." *Dis wok na hoday somting.* (This work not whole day something.) "This work is not something that will take all day."

**hold**: [hol] *v.,* To accept. *If A gii yu hundreh dala for de ting, yu will hole ih?* (If I give you hundred dollar for the thing, you will hold it?) "If I give you one hundred dollars for it, will you accept?"

**hold word**: [ho wɔ] *v.,* To hold off on pronouncing one's opinion or judgment on a matter. *De woman fini tok de case, buh fo na A will hold word.* (The woman finish talk the case, but for now I will hold word.) "The woman has explained her side of the story, but for now I will wait before giving my opinion." See **break word**.

**hole yo foot**: [hol yo fʊtˀ] "hold your foot" *v.*, A figurative expression meaning "to humbly ask." In extreme cases Liberians might actually grasp the foot of their patron to indicate their servile position. *A beg yu ma man, A need small money. A hole yo foot.* (I beg you, my man. I need small money. I hold your foot.) "Could you please give me a little cash? I humbly ask you."

**hole yo heart**: [hol yo ha:tˀ] "hold your heart" *idiom.*, Be patient. Just wait a little. *Hole yo heart pekin. Yo ma coming jus na.* (Hold your heart pekin. Your ma coming just now.) "Be patient little boy. Your mom will be here soon."

**hole-hole**: [holɪholɪ] "hold it, hold it" *n*, A passenger bus. *De taxi wa all pack, buh A fine one hole-hole to carry me Broad Street.* (The taxi was all pack, but I find one holdit-holdit to carry me Broad Street.) "The taxis were all full, but I found a bus to take me to Broad Street."

**Holy Mary**: [holi meɹi] *n.,*, A pejorative term for a girl who seeks to uphold a high moral standard against negative peer pressure. Similar to the American expressions "holier than thou" and "goody two-shoes." *Da Holy Mary tell me say she won look for gohfada.* (That Holy Mary tell me say she won't look for godfather.) "That goody two-shoes told me she won't look for a sugardaddy.

**honorable**: [haneɹabʌ] *adj.*, An honorific title given to government officials. The "H" is strongly emphasized in the pronunciation. *One honorable will be to Bopolu fo de graduation.* (One honorable will be to Bopolu for the graduation.) "One esteemed government official will be in Bopolu for the graduation ceremony."

**hope**: [hop] v., To think, believe. *A hope she will come tomorrow.* (I hope she will come tomorrow.) "I believe she will come tomorrow."

**hot**: [hatˀ] *v.*, To heat. *De woman hot wata fo hur husban so he cu tek baf.* (The woman hot water for her husband so he could take bath.) "The woman heated water for her husband so he could bathe." For the state of being hot, see **heateh**.

**human being**: [hjumɔ̃ bĭ] *n.*, 1. A person. This term is used much more frequently in Liberian English than Standard English. *Da man monkey can be acting lek real human being.* (That man monkey can be acting like real human being.) "That guy's monkey acts just like a person." 2. Man, mankind. *Human being can alway be giving deh fren hard tam.* (Human being can be giving their friend hard time.) "People are always causing problems for one another."

**humbug**: [hʌmbɔ] *v.*, To bother, pester, annoy. *Hoday da man can be humbugging de chief fo hih lan bisneh.* (Whole day that man can be humbugging the chief for his land business.) "That man is always bothering the chief about his land issue."

**hungry food**: [hʌ̃gɹi fu] *n.,* Non-preferred crops or wild foods such as **hungry rice, bush yam** and **palm cabbage** that are eaten in times of scarcity.

**hungry rice**: [hʌ̃gɹi ɹaɪs] n., Millet, also known as **foni**. *Digitaria exilis.* A common grain in savanna regions, millet is occasionally grown in Liberia as a rice substitute, although it is not preferred.

**hungry tam**: [hʌ̃gɹi tam] "hungry time" *n.,* Although this term may be used in general reference to a famine, it is most often used to mean an annual period of time during the rainy season in which farmers wait for the new harvest of rice, while last year's store is depleted. During this time Liberians may be forced to eat **hungry food**.

**hus boy**: [hɑs bɔɪ] "house boy" *n.,* A male household worker.

**hus geh**: [hɑs gɛ] "house girl" *n.,* A female household worker.

**hus lizay**: [hus leze] "house lizard" *n.,* The common house gecko. *Hemidactylus frenatus.* These are popularly believed to cause bald spots on peoples' heads by spitting on them. They are also known by a number of other names such as *white lizard, paparoni* and *six o'clock. Deh one hus lizay on de wall.* (There one house lizard on the wall.) "There is a house gecko on the wall."

**hustle**: [hʌso] *v.,* To work hard to provide for yourself. *Ih na been easy since my ma die. A jus been hustling fo mysef.* (It not been easy since my ma die. I just been hustling for myself.) "It's been hard since my mom died. I've just been working hard to try to make ends meet.

# I

**icebox:** [aɪs bas] *n.*, Used rather than "refrigerator" or "freezer." *Yu can plea pu de soft drink eenside de icebox so ih can be getting co?* (You can please put the soft drink inside the icebox so it can be getting cold.) "Could you please put the soft drinks in the refrigerator so they'll get cold?"

**identico:** [aɪdɛ̃tiko] "identical" *adj.*, Exact, particular. *Da dis identico woman wa wa to de shop dis moning.* (That this identical woman what was to the shop this morning.) "It was that exact woman who was at the store this morning."

**ifan:** [ɪfã] "if" *conj.*, Used to indicate the conditions which must happen for a certain outcome to take place. *Ifan yu wan carry de cycle, yu muh bring de balance money.* (If you want carry the cycle, you must bring the balance money.) "If you want to take the bicycle, you need to bring the rest of the money."

**ineh:** [ĩnɪ] "isn't it" 1. Question particle. Can be placed at the beginning or end of a sentence when anticipating a positive response. *De papay die ever since, ineh?* (The papay die ever since, isn't it?) "The old man died a long time ago, didn't he?" *Ineh yo uncu Mr. Cooper?* (Isn't your uncle Mr. Cooper?) "Isn't Mr. Cooper your uncle?" 2. Can also be used in response to a surprising statement, similar to 'Is that so?' in Standard English.

**injeshun:** [ĩd͡ʒɛʃɔ̃] "injection" *n.*, Used rather than "shot." *A go to de docta an he gii me tdee injeshun.* (I go to the doctor and he give me three injection.) "I went to the doctor and he gave me three shots." See also **drip.**

**inpen:** [ĩpɛ̃] "ink pen" *n.*, Used rather than "pen." *A loss my inpen. Ifan you fine ih, yu muh plea tell me, yah?* (I lost my ink pen. If you find it, you must please tell me, hear?) "I've lost my pen. If you find it, could you please tell me?"

**interior:** [ĩtijɔ] *n.*, Refers to the inland regions of Liberia away from the coast. Formerly called the **hinterland.**

**Irish potato:** [aɪɪʃ poteto] *n.*, Used for imported potatoes rather than local sweet potato varieties.

**iron:** [ajõ] 1. *n.*, Often used in a more general sense to refer to any metal such as iron, aluminum or steel. 2. *adj.*, Hard, firm. *Ma husban leave me fo one nyoung geh wa geh iron tete.* (My husband leave me for one young girl what get iron tete.) "My husband left me for a young girl with firm breasts."

**iron soap**: [ajõ sop] *n.,* Locally produced soap. Cheap, but hard on clothes. *Dey coming show we de women ha to fis iron soap.* (They coming show we the women how to fix iron soap.) "They are going to show us women how to make homemade soap."

**issue**: [ɪʃu] *n.,* 1. Distributed relief goods. *Wen de NGO fini giving de man hih issue, he go sell ih skrate.* (When the NGO finish giving the man his issue, he go sell it straight.) "After the NGO gave the man his relief goods, he sold them right away." 2. Dog meat. A common food during the civil war. Slang. *A wan eat some issue, but to fine ih na easy.* (I want eat some issue, but to find it not easy.) "I want to eat some dog meat, but it's not easy to find now."

# J

**jack** (1): [d͡ʒæk˺] *n.*, Someone who is tricky or clever in manipulating situations. From the **tricky jack** or **rabbit** character in traditional folk tales. *Yu betta tek tam wif da man; he's a real jack.* (You better take time with that man; he's a real jack.) "Watch out for that guy: he's a real trickster."

**jack** (2): [d͡ʒæk˺] *n.*, The Variegated Grasshopper. *Zonocerus Variegatus.* A large, slow moving grasshopper with a foul odor. Green and yellow in color. A common pest. Considered by some Liberians to be a delicacy.

**jacko:** [d͡ʒakɔ] "jackal" *n.*, The Mangabey Monkey. *Cerceocebus torquatus atys.* A small grey monkey with white eyelids and long tail. Commonly kept as a pet. *Mamadi buy one jacko to be carboy fo heen.* (Mamadi buy one jacko to be carboy for him.) "Mamadi bought a jackal monkey to be his car boy."

**jahfeh:** [d͡ʒafɛ] *n.*, Slang term for money. From the Vai language. *Ba, gii me small jahfeh leh me go buy sof drink.* (Ba, give me small jahfeh let me go buy soft drink.) "Buddy, give me a little money to go buy some soda."

**jaja:** [d͡ʒad͡ʒa] *n.*, Insignificant, meaningless. *Da na jaja ting A doing yeh.* (This not jaja thing I doing here.) "This isn't a meaningless thing I'm doing here." See also **fekehfekeh**.

**jam:** [d͡ʒæm] 1. *adj.*, To be in a difficult situation. *A rally jam since de papay go Ghana.* (I really jam since the papay go Ghana.) "I've been really in a bind since the old man went to Ghana." 2. *v.*, To pressure. *Don jam me fo money bisneh.* (Don't jam me for money business.) "Don't pressure me for money."

**jap:** [d͡ʒaɪp] *v.*, 1. To cheat, fool. May be derived from the Standard English "jip." *Eh my man, ha yu wan jap me so?* (Hey, my man, how you want jap me so?) "Hey buddy, why are you trying to cheat me like that?" 2. To joke. *Yu say my motobike geh missing? A hope yu na japping me!* (You say my motorbike get missing? I hope you not japping me!) "You said you lost my motorbike? You better not be kidding me!"

**jealous:** [d͡ʒɛləs] *v.*, To feel envious of another's good fortune. Whereas in Standard English this word is an adjective, it is more commonly used as a verb in Liberian English. *De tam Lorpu see Hawa nyew baby, she jealous hur.* (The time Lorpu see Hawa new baby, she jealous her.) "When Lorpu saw Hawa's new baby, she was jealous of her."

**jigga:** [d͡ʒigə] "jigger" *n.*, A species of flea, *Tunga penetrans,* known for burrowing into the flesh of the foot. (Also called "chigoe flea" in other countries.) *Jigga quick to enta yo foot ifan yu ain wear slippa.* (Jigger quick to enter your foot if you ain't wear slipper.) "You will get jiggers soon if you don't wear flip-flops."

**jike**: [d͡ʒaɪkˑ] "jerk" v., 1. To pull quickly. *De fish wa jiking me.* (The fish was jerking me.) The fish was tugging my line." 2. To be shocked by electricity. *De current jike me ba way.* (The current jerk me bad way.) "The electricity shocked me terribly."

**jimmyjohn**: [d͡ʒɪmid͡ʒã] *n.,* A large barrel. *A buy one jimmyjohn to Red Light to haul my red oil.* (I buy one jimmyjohn to Red Light to haul my red oil.) "I bought a barrel in Red Light to transport my red oil."

**jina**: [d͡ʒina] *n.,* A genie. Spirit beings that may manifest themselves in physical forms. Commonly believed to live in rivers, mountains, and the forest. From the Arabic *jinn* via the Mandingo language. *De jina grap de man and carry him una de wata.* (The jina grab the man and carry him under the water.) "The genie grabbed the man and pulled him under the water."

**job**: [d͡ʒab] *v.,* To work. *A jobbing to City Bank na.* (I jobbing to City Bank now.) "I am working at City Bank now."

**join**: [d͡ʒõj] *v.,* To fuse. *Doh tdee tree join togeda.* (Those three tree join together.) "Those three trees fused together."

**joke-mate**: [d͡ʒok metˑ] *n.,* A person of a certain clan with whom your clan has a joking relationship. In Liberia the Mandingo especially are known for having joke-mates. A person upon introduction to their joke-mate may say something that would sound extremely derogatory or insulting to an outsider such as, "So you're a Kromah? I know you all are a bunch of good for nothing thieves!" or "The Kamaras were our slaves. Slave, go fetch me some water or I will beat you!" The joke-mate will recognize the relationship, laugh, and then return the insult. *De Kromah dem awa joke-mates. We can cauz dem an dey will jus laugh.* (The Kromah them our joke-mates. We can curse them and they will just laugh.) "The Kromahs are our joke-mates. We can insult them and they will just laugh.

**jollof rice**: [d͡ʒaləf raɪs] *n.,* A common dish in Liberia made from rice, meat, vegetables, and tomato sauce. Commonly eaten on special occasions such as graduations or weddings. *Jollof rice sweet wif chicken meat.* (Jollof rice sweet with chicken meat.) "Jollof rice is tasty with chicken meat."

**ju**: [d͡ʒu] "jewel" *n.,* A sweetheart, lover. *Me and my ju jus na coming fron de video club.* (Me and my jewel just now coming from the video club.) "My girlfriend and I just came from the video club."

**juju**: [d͡ʒud͡ʒu] *n.,* A disparaging term for occultic practices and paraphernalia. For a positive sense Liberians usually use the word **medicine**.

**juju man**: [d͡ʒud͡ʒu mɛ̃] *n.,* A witchdoctor. Usually used in a pejorative sense. See also **zoe** and **moliman**. *De juju man tell hur say she muh kill one white chicken.* (The juju man tell her say she must kill one white chicken.) "The witchdoctor told her that she should kill a white chicken."

**juke**: [d͡ʒukʼ] *v.,* 1. To poke, pierce, puncture. *De fish torn juke my finga.* (The fish thorn juke my finger.) "The fish bone pierced my finger." 2. To steal, con. *If yu ain tek tam da katakata man coming juke yu out of plenty money.* (If you ain't take time that katakata man coming juke you out of plenty money.) "If you aren't careful that trickster will con you out of a lot of money."

**junshun**: [d͡ʒʌ̃ʃʌ̃] "junction" *n.,* Used rather than "intersection" or "corner." *A wan drop to de junshun.* (I want drop to the junction.) "I want to get down at the intersection."

**jus lek**: [d͡ʒɛs laɪkʼ] "just like" *adj.,* Used more often than "the same as." *Ma owna cycle jus lek yo own.* (My own of cycle just like your own.) "My bike is the same as yours."

**jus na**: [d͡ʒɛs na] "just now" *adv.,* Right away. *Plea wait small, A coming jus na.* (Please wait small. I coming just now.) "Please wait a bit. I'm coming right away."

# K

**kafu:** [kafu] *n.*, A herbal potion or "medicine" used in trial by ordeal in interior courts. It is placed on the tongue of the witness before a testimony is given. Should the witness lie, the kafu is believed to harm or kill the person. From the Kpelle language. See also **sassywood**.

**kalabuley:** [kalabule] *adj.*, Fake, imitation. *Da so so kalabuley wristwatch he wa selling.* (That so so kilabuley wristwatch he was selling.) "He was only selling fakes wristwatches." See also **colloma**.

**kalla:** [kala] *n.*, Doughnuts fried in oil. *Yeh de place weh all de women dem can be fising kalla een de morning.* (Here the place where all the women them can be fixing kalla in the morning.) "Here's where all the woman make doughnuts in the morning."

**kanki:** [kãki] *n.*, A Liberian measurement of rice, equivalent to one Liberian cup or two American cups. See also **cup, tin** and **kroo**.

**karmo:** [ka:mo] *n.*, An Islamic cleric and teacher, often skilled in the art of making Qur'anic charms. From the Mandingo language *karãmɔɔ* "teacher." Similar to the **moliman**, although the karmo's primary role is that of a teacher.

**katakata:** [katakata] 1. *adj.*, Tricky, mischievous. *Da katakata man always running behind money bisneh.* (That katakata man always running behind money business.) "That scam artist is always looking to find money." 2. *n.*, A scheme, con, a mischievous action. *A don wan Moses to play katakata on me.* (I don't want Moses to play katakata on me.) "I don't want Moses to con me."

**kayan:** [kajã] *n.*, A crumbly snack made of rice, sugar and peanut butter.

**keenu:** [kinu] *n.*, A dugout canoe. *A ain brave to siddon eenside da keenu.* (I ain't brave to sit down inside that canoe.) "I'm not brave enough to sit inside that canoe."

**keep comping:** [ki kɔŋpiŋ] "keep company" *v.*, To visit. *We come to keep company.* (We come to keep company.) "We've come to visit."

**keeping:** [kipī] *n.*, Used rather than "feeling" or "doing" in enquiries about one's health. *Ha yu been keeping?* (How you been keeping?) "How have you been doing?"

**kesh har tam:** [kɛʃ ha: tam] "catch hard time" *v.*, To experience problems or difficulties. *A rally been keshing har tam dee few days.* (I really been catching hard time these few days.) "I've really been struggling recently."

97

**kesh heh:** [heʃ hɛ] "catch head" *v.*, To get drunk. *Erasmas go kesh heh to de cane juice shop.* (Erasmas go catch head to the cane juice shop.) "Erasmas went and got drunk at the cane liquor shop."

**kill fish:** [kɪ fiʃ] "kill fish" *v.*, In Liberia people do not "catch" fish, rather they "kill fish." There is no concept of "catch and release." *A wa coming kill plenty fish, buh my catguh cut.* (I was coming kill plenty fish, but my cat-gut cut.) "I was going to catch a lot of fish, but my line broke."

**kinja:** [kĩd͡ʒa] *n.*, A make-shift basket with shoulder straps and a headband. Woven from oil palm fronds and used to carry meat or produce from the bush into the village. *De tam he fini cutting palm nut he fis kinja to haul ih een town.* (The time he finish cutting palm nut he fix kinja to haul it in town.) "After he cut the palm nuts, he wove a kinja to transport them to town."

**king monkey:** [kiŋ mɔkɛ] *n.*, The Diana Monkey. *Cercopithecus Diana Diana.* A large colorful monkey. Also called **dandy jack**.

**kingay:** [kiŋge] *n.*, Ringworm. Often seen as a white, bald patch on children's heads. *Ma pa say we muh tek tam so da white lizay cyan spit on uh an gii uh heh kingay.* (My pa say we must take time so that white lizard can't spit on us and give us head kingay.) "My father said we should be careful that those house geckos don't spit on us and give us ringworm on our heads."

**kishen:** [kiʃi] "Kitchen" *n.*, 1. Small, makeshift shelters built on farms to protect farmers from the sun and rain. *Wen he fini brushing de farm, he will fis de kishen.* (When he finish brushing the farm, he will fix the kitchen.) "When he is done clearing the farm, he will build the shelter." 2. A stilted structure built next to houses in villages. Used to store rice and other produce. *Ma rice kishen fulluh na.* (My rice kitchen full up now.) "My rice shed is full now." 3. A market stall. *De tam my moda drive me fron de hus A nyuse to sleep una de markeh kishen.* (The time my mother drive me from the house I used to sleep under the market kitchen.) "When my mother drove me from the house I slept under the market stalls."

**Kissi:** [kisi] *n.*, A people group from the Foya district of Lofa County in northwestern Liberia. They speak a language in the Atlantic family. Population is approximately 115,000 in Liberia. Also found in Sierra Leone and Guinea. Primarily animistic and Christian.

**kissi penny:** [kisi peni] *n.*, See **country money**.

**kissme:** [kɪs mi] "kiss meat" *n.*, A small snail that lives in brackish-water coastal swamps. Collected for food. Named for the kissing noise that results from sucking the meat from the shell. *A buy some kissme een de* *markeh to fis wif palm butta.* (I buy some kissmeat in the market to fix with palm butter.) "I bought some kiss meat in the market to make with palm butter."

**kitili**: [kɪtili] *n.,* Small round vegetables with a bitter taste. Green or red in color. Added to sauces for flavor. *Yu wan so A muh puh kitili in de soup fo you?* (You want so I must put kitili in the soup for you?) "Do you want me to put kitili in the soup for you?"

**knock belly**: [nak bɛli] *idiom.,* To give a gift or service to another as motivation for carrying out a requested service. A bribe. See also **kola, co wata, respect,** and **scratch back.**

**knock off**: [nak ɔf] *v.,* To quit working, to call it a day. *Ih five o'clock na. Leh knock off.* (It five o'clock now. Let knock off.) "It's five o'clock now. Let's call it a day."

**kola**: [kola] *n.,* 1. A red or white nut of the *Cola nitida* tree. There are two kinds of kola: "bitter" kola and "sweet" kola. "Sweet" kola is only slightly less bitter. Chewed as a stimulant and appetite suppressant. Also used in ceremonial gift exchanges. White kola symbolizes purity of heart and good intention. Kola is also used as sacrifice in sacred rituals. *De zoe say she muh leave ten kola una de cotton tree.* (The zoe say she must leave ten kola under the cotton tree.) "The zoe said she should leave ten kola nuts under the cotton tree." 2. "Kola" may also be used as a euphemism for a bribe. *De offica to de gate say we muh give heen small kola befo we pass.* (The officer to the gate say we must give him small kola before we pass.) "The officer at the checkpoint said we should give him a little money if we want him to let us through."

**koningi**: [koniŋgi] n., A traditional stringed instrument. Rare today, but formerly common throughout Liberia. Consists of a triangular frame with 6-8 wire strings mounted to a calabash gourd. *Da ole man can ring the koningi fine!* (The old man can ring the koning fine!) That old man plays the koning very well!" May also be called **country guita.**

**kongo**: [kõŋgo] *n.,* An annex built on an existing house. *A coming fis kongo on my house so anytam stranga come dey can sleep deh.* (I coming fix kongo on my house so anytime stranger come they can sleep there.) "I am going to build an annex on my house so anytime visitors come they can sleep there."

**kongoma**: [kɔ̃ŋgoma] *n.,* A large thumb piano. Constructed from a plywood with three tines made from saw blades.

**kor**: [kɔ] *n.,* Points scored in the girl's stomping and clapping rhythm game called **nafu.**

**kpaka**: [k͡paka] *n.,* Rhinoceros beetle. See **gbagon.**

**kpaku**: [k͡paku] *adj.*, Slim, small for one's size.

**kpamgba (1)**: [k͡pamg͡ba] *n.*, A kind of dried fish.

**kpamgba (2)**: [k͡pamg͡ba] *v.*, To make medicine, cast a spell. *A pay one ole man to kpamgba dis woman palava.* (I pay one old man to kpamgba this woman palaver.) "I paid an old man to cast a spell over my woman troubles."

**kpamgba man**: [k͡pamg͡ba mã] *n.*, A medicine man, sorcerer. *Deh one kpamgba man to de village wa can solve yo prorem.* (There one kpamgba man to the village what can solve your problem.) "There is a medicine man in Koli Town who can solve your problem.

**Kpelle**: [k͡pɛle] *n.*, The largest people group in Liberia. Speak a Southwest-Mande language. Population is approximately 490,000. Located primarily in Bong and Lofa Counties. Also present in Southern Guinea where they are known as the Guerze. Primarily practitioners of African traditional religion and Christianity, although certain sections have a sixable Muslim population.

**Krahn**: [kɹã] *n.*, A group of related Kwa-speaking ethnic groups of southeastern Liberia and western Ivory Coast, numbering approximately 100,000. Similarly to the Grebo, for politically expediency the Liberian government grouped these tribes together in the later half of the 20th century. Some of these divisions include the Tchien, Tepo and Sapo. Although their cultures are related, their languages are not necessarily mutually intelligible. Primarily Christian and animistic.

**krokroji**: [kɹokɹod͡ʒi] *adj.*, Shady practices, corruption. Perhaps from Standard English "crooked deeds." *Eman can chop plenty wif hih krokroji bisneh.* (Eman can chop plenty with his krokroji business.) "Emanuel embezzles a lot of money with his shady business dealings."

**kroo**: [kɹu] *n.*, A measurement for dry goods, similar to the English "bushel." Equivalent to roughly ten bundles of cut rice or three to five tins of threshed rice.

**Kru**: [kɹu] *n.*, A grouping of Kwa-speaking tribes native to south-eastern Liberia, numbering approximately 270,000. Many Kru make their living on the sea as fisherman. During colonial times the Kru were often recruited by Europeans as deck hands on their merchant vessels. The largest subsection includes the Klao and Tajuasohn. Primarily Christian and animistic.

**Kru keenu**: [kɹu kinu] "Kru canoe" *n.*, Refers to a small, one person dugout canoe. Used on the ocean.

**kubba**: [kuba] *adj.*, A master, expert. Slang usage. *Sekou da real kubba driva.* (Sekou that real kubba driver.) "Sekou is a master driver."

**kukujumuku**: [kukujumuku] *idiom.*, Inside knowledge, a secret shared by members of the same group. *Why yu aksing plenty queshion? Dih ting da kukujumuku; yu na eenside yu na know.* (Why are you asking so many questions? This thing that kukujumuku; you not inside you not know.) "Why are you asking so many questions? If you aren't on the inside, you won't understand what I am talking about."

**kuu**: [ku:] *n.*, 1. A rotational savings club. Members put money into a pool from which they borrow in turn. From the Kpelle language. See also **susu**. 2. A cooperative in which farmers pool their labor by scheduling alternating workdays on member's farms. Primarily active in the labor-intensive periods at the beginning and end of the farming season. *We de farma dem can mek kuu fo de haves tam.* (We the farmer them can make kuu for the harvest time.) "We the farmers pool our labor for the harvest time."

**kuway**: [kuwe] "Kool-Aid" *n.*, 1. A sour milk drink frozen and sold in small plastic bags. *Korpu been fising kuway to sell een de markeh. (Korpu been fixing kuway to sell in the market.)* "Korpu has been making sour-milk to sell in the market." 2. This term may also be used more broadly as a generic term for any sweetened beverage.

**kwi**: [kwi] *adj.*, Civilized, Western. Used by tribal peoples to refer to all things non-indigenous, including people. Applied to Americans, Europeans, Americo-Liberians, or even tribal people who have adopted Western ways. From the Kpelle language. *Doh kwi peepo ain love too mush oh red oil.* (Those kwi people ain't love too much of red oil.) "Those civilized people don't like a lot of red oil (in their food)." See also **civilize**.

# L

**LAMCO**: [lamkɔ] *n.*, The Liberian American-Swedish Minerals Company. LAMCO formally ran a large mining operation near Yekepa in Nimba County. Their facilities were looted during the war and the company is now defunct.

**lanlaw**: [lãlɔ] "landlord" *n.*, Also called *hus owna* (house owner).

**lappa**: [lapa] *n.*, African cloth. Bright in color and sold in two yard lengths. Commonly wrapped around the waist and worn as a skirt by women. Also used to carry babies on the back. *A wan back de baby wif de lappa. You muh plea help me, yah?* (I want back the baby with the lappa. You must please help me, you hear?) "I want to tie the baby on my back with the African cloth. Could you please help me?"

**lappalonian**: [lapaloniã] *adj.*, A pejorative term used of women who chose to dress in traditional attire rather than Western clothing.

**lappa suit**: [lapa su] *n.*, A fancy outfit for woman made from **lappa** cloth. *De tailor fini sew one fine lappa suit fo me.* (The tailor finish sew one fine lappa suit for me.) "The tailor sewed a very nice lappa suit for me."

**larry**: [leɹi] *adj.*, 1. Crazy. *De witchcraft mek heen larry.* (The witchcraft make him larry.) "The witchcraft made him crazy." 2. Close-minded. *Da larry geh still tink she een de bush.* (The larry girl still think she in the bush.) "That close-minded girl still thinks she's living in the village."

**las price**: [las pɹaɪs] "last price" *n.*, A phrase used when dickering to indicate the lowest amount one is willing to pay. Often however the "last price" can be reduced even further with additional bantering.

**lasmo**: [lasmo] *n.*, A small talismen worn on the arm or waist for protection. Made by Muslim clerics from a passage of the Koran written on a scrap of paper and sewn into a leather pouch. See also **moliman**.

**las tam**: [las tam] *n.*, The other day, before. *A gii yu de copybook las tam.* (I give you the copybook last time.) "I gave you the copybook the other day."

**laugh**: [laf] *v.*, To smile. *Yor muh laugh wen he taking de photo.* (Y'all must laugh when he taking the photo.) "You all should smile when he is taking the picture."

**law**: [lau] *n.* 1. An edict or rule. Often refers to those issued by tribal leaders. *We get law yeh say no woman muh enta dis forest.* (We get law here say no woman must enter the forest.) "We have a law here that says no women are allowed to enter this forest." 2. A taboo. Liberians in tribal communities traditionally have strong taboos prohibiting them from eating certain animals and some vegetables. These are often passed along clan lines. Many have myths about how a certain animal saved the ancestor of the clan and thus a pact was made with them. *Awa great-granfada wa loss in de bush wen pokipine show him de ro to de village. Da why he say da awa law na to eat dis meat.* (Our great-grandfather was lost in the bush when porcupine show him the road to the village. That why he say that our law not to eat this meat.) "When our great-grandfather was lost in the woods, a porcupine showed him the road to the village. That's why he said we should not eat this kind of animal."

**lazy:** [lesi] *adj.*, Weak, lacking strength. Does not necessarily imply slothfulness as in Standard English. *Stephen lazy. Hih lil broda sef abo heen.* (Stephen lazy. His little brother self able him.) "Stephen is weak. Even his little brother can take him on."

**LD:** [ɛl di] *n.*, See **Liberty**.

**leave:** [lif] *v.*, to stay, remain. *De tam dey wa going to de farm A leave behine.* (The time they was going to the farm I leave behind.) "When they went to the farm I stayed behind."

**leave small:** [lif smau] *adv.*, Almost. *My money leave small to fini.* (My money leave small to finish.) "My money is almost gone."

**leh ih stay:** [lɛ ɪ stej] "let it stay" *idiom.*, To overlook an offence. Used rather than, "Forget about it", "Drop it" etc. *A know Mulbah say ru ting to yu, buh A beg yu jus leh ih stay.* (I know Mulbah say rude thing to you, but I beg you just let it stay.) "I know Mulbah said something rude to you, but please just forget about it."

**lemon:** [lɛmõ] *n.*, May be used in reference to a tangerine. See **lime**.

**lepor:** [lɛpɔ] "leopard" *n,*. The leopard. *Felis pardus reichenow*i. A large spotted feline found in Liberian forests. Greatly feared by common people, but sought after by hunters for their valuable skin and teeth.

**lepor fish:** [lɛpɔ fiʃ] "leopard fish" *n.*, The African Pike Characin. *Hepsetus odoe.* A predatory fish with sharp teeth. May reach lengths of up to three feet. Also know as **dog fish** in some parts of Liberia.

**Lepor Society:** [lɛpɔ sosaɪti] "Leopard Society" *n.*, A secretive occultic organization whose members believed themselves able to transform into leopards. They disguised ritualistic murders as leopard attacks. Apparently defunct after being suppressed by the Liberian government in the mid 19th century, although ritualistic murders continue to be a problem. See **heart man**.

**lesher:** [lɛʃɔ] "lecture" *v.*, Casual conversation, chit-chat. Does not imply a formal discourse. *A wan so yu muh come to my hus so we can be lesher-*

104

*ing.* (I want so you must come to my house so we can be lecturing.) "I would like you to come over to my house sometime so we can chat."

**Liberian white man**: [laɪbiɹ̃ɛ̃ waɪ mɛ̃] *n.*, An albino person. *"Liberian white man cyan staylohn een de sun."* (Liberian white man can't stay long in the sun.) "An albino can't last out in the sun."

**Liberty**: [lɪbati] *n.*, The Liberian dollar currency. Often called **LD** for short. Has denominations of 5, 10, 20, and 100. As of 2011, the exchange rate is approximately 70 Liberty to 1 U.S. dollar.

**lie**: [laɪ] *n.*, False information, whether given intentional or not. *Da lie!* "That's a lie" is a phrase very commonly used in Liberian English. This term should not be necessarily understood as a serious accusation of lying. A closer meaning would be "That's not true." *Yu say my fren go een town? Da lie! Deh heen deh.* (You say my friend go in town? That lie! There him there.) "You said my friend went in town. That's not true! He's over there."

**lie-lie**: [laɪ laɪ] *adj.*, Lying. *A ain know why Momo can be behine da lie-lie woman.* (I ain't know why Momo can be behind that lie-lie woman.) "I don't know why Momo goes after that lying woman."

**Lightning Society**: [laɪm̃ɪ sosaɪti] *n.*, A secretive organization whose members are believed to be able harness the power of lightning through sorcery, causing it to strike intended victims.

**lime**: [lã] *n.*, Small citrus fruit, including limes and lemons.

**lion**: [liõ] *n.*, Although lions do not exist in Liberia, this term is sometimes used to refer to the leopard. See **lepor**.

**lion monkey**: [liõ mõkɛ] *n.*, May refer to the King Colobus (*Colobus ploykomos*) or the Red Colobus (*Piliocolobus badius*) monkeys. Both are medium sized monkeys that have a reddish coat with white markings.

**lo**: [lo] "load" *n.*, Baggage, items to be transported. *Dey fini pack my lo on de hole-hole.* (They finish pack my load on the holdit-holdit.) "They already packed my bags on the bus."

**lock** (1): [lakˀ] *v.*, To set a trap. *A can lock hook in dis wata, buh since las week A cyan kesh noting.* (I can lock hook in this water, but since last week I can't catch nothing.) "I leave baited hooks in this creek, but I haven't caught anything since last week."

**lock** (2): [lakˀ] *adj.*, To be full (with food.) Slang. *Ma man, A lock.* (My man, I lock.) "Buddy, I can't eat another bite."

**long**: [lɔ̃] *adj.*, In additional to the Standard English usage, "long" may be used by some Liberian English speakers to mean "tall." Many indigenous Liberian languages do not distinguish "tall" and "long."

**long devil**: [lɔ̃ dɛwo] *n.*, A masked dancer on stilts. Most commonly associated with the Gio ethnic group. Often seen at festivals accompanied by an entourage of drummers. See also **devil**. *De long devil fini dancing. Den he siddon owa de car.* (The long devil finish dancing. Then he sit down over the car.) "The stilted dancer finished dancing. Then he sat down on the car."

**look**: [lʊkˀ] *v.*, 1. To see (figuratively), to think about. *Ha yu look ah Cecelia prorem?* (How you look at Cecelia problem?) "What do you think about Cecelia's problem?" 2. To possess certain attributes. Can be used about a person. *A ain easy to vex. Da jus ha A looking.* (I ain't easy to vex. That just how I looking.) "It is hard for me to get mad. That's just the way I am." 3. To appear in a certain manner. *Dis lil geh looking too fine today!* (This little girl looking too fine today!) "That little girl looks very nice today." 4. To seem like, as if. *Ih looking lek ih wan rain.* (It looking like it want rain.) "It seems as if it is going to rain."

**looking fo ih**: [lʊkĩ fo ɪ] "looking for it" *v.*, To "ask for it," to bring punishment upon one's self. *Newa mine da geh. She wa looking fo ih.* (Never mind the girl. She was looking for it.) "Don't worry about her. She was asking for it."

**looking glass**: [lʊkĩ glæs] *n.*, Often used to mean "mirror."

**loose**: [lus] *v.*, To untie, loosen. *Why na yu loose da chicken?* (Why not you loose that chicken?) "Why don't you untie that chicken."

**Lorma**: [lɔ:ma] *n.*, A Southwest-Mande speaking ethnic group native to Lofa County. Population is approximately 165,000. Formally called the Buzzi, this term is now seen as being a pejorative. Also present in Guinea where they are known as Toma. Primarily animistic with some Christian presence.

**loss**: [lɔs] "lost" *v.*, To be lost, missing. Most often heard as an active rather than passive verb. *Ma I.D. card loss las ni.* (My I.D. card loss last night.) "My I.D. card got lost last night."

**lova**: [lʌwa] "lover" *n.*, An unmarried sexual partner.

**love medicine**: [lʌv mɛɾəsĩ] "love medicine" *n.*, A potion designed to cause a one person to fall in love with another.

**loving**: [lʌvĩ] *v.*, To engage in illicit sexual activity. *He de one wa can be loving to da geh.* (He the one what can be loving to that girl.) "He is the one who has been sleeping with that girl."

**lucky ticket**: [lʌki tikɛ] *n.,* 1. A game of chance, a lottery. 2. A chance occurrence. *To geh visa to de U.S., da jus lucky ticket. (To get visa to the U.S., that just lucky ticket.)* "Getting a visa for the U.S. is like winning the lottery."

**ludo**: [ludo] *n.,* A simple board game popular in Liberia. The playing surface is usually under glass in a small wooden frame. Played with two die and plastic markers.

**LURD**: [lɛɹd] *n.,* Liberians United for Reconciliation and Democracy. A rebel faction, an offshoot of ULIMO, that played a major part in the last part of the Liberian civil war. Comprised mainly of Mandingos.

# M

**ma**: [ma] *n.*, 1. A mother. *My ma born five chiren.* (My ma born five children.) "My mother gave birth to five children." 2. A term of respect for older woman. *Hello ma, ha yu been keeping?"* (Hello ma, how you been keeping.) "Hello ma'am, how have you been?"

**magazine**: [magazĩ] *n.*, Almost always refers to a cartridge of ammunition, not a literary publication. For this see **pamfleh**.

**mala**: [mala] *n.*, Melegueta pepper. *Aframomum melegueta.* A spice in the ginger family. In former times the trade in Malagueta pepper led European sailors to call Liberia the "Pepper Coast." Liberians today eat the interior pulp and seeds of the raw pods and used the dried seeds for tea and medicinal purposes. Occasionally called **alligata peppa**.

**mamie-wata**: [mami wata] *n.*, A mermaid spirit believed to inhabit rivers, lakes and the ocean. Some view her as a source of evil, while others seek her power in gaining wealth. *Da man dealing wif one mamie-wata. Da wa mek ih he reesh so.* (The man dealing with one mamie-wata. That what make it he rich so.) "The reason that man is rich is because he engaged in witchcraft with a mermaid."

**man**: [mɛ̃] *adj.*, 1. Relating to the male gender. Used for animals as well as humans. *Deh one man cow stanning to de football fiel.* (The one man cow standing to the football field.) "That's a bull standing in the soccer field." 2. An informal address which can be applied to anyone, male of female. *Ma man, yu muh na humbug me so.* (My man, you must not humbug me so.) "Buddy, you shouldn't bother me like that."

**manage**: [mænæʒ] *v.*, To be able to. *Ha da dog manage to steal de meat?* (How the dog manage to steal the meat?) "How was that dog able to steal the meat?"

**man bush**: [mɛ̃ buɪʃ] *n.*, The Poro grove. *No one can say wa dey fini toking on een de man bush.* (No one can say what they finish talking on in the man bush.) "No one can say what they were talking about in the Poro grove." See **Poro**.

**Mandingo**: [mæ̃diŋgo] *n.*, A Liberian ethnic group that speaks a Northern Mande language. There are two main divisions of Mandingo in Liberia, the Konyaka and the Manya. The Konyaka are primarily known as merchants and mechanics and have no territory in Liberia. The Manya of Lofa County live primarily as subsistence farmers. Other non-native Mande peoples such as the Maninka and Bambara from Guinea and Mali may also be referred to as Mandingos. Because of their Islamic religion and cultural differences, as well as their perceived monopoly in business, the Mandingos are often marginalized. Total population in Liberia is approximately 100,000.

**mango fly:** [mẽgo flaɪ] *n.*, The botfly. Infamous for laying their eggs on human skin. The larvae develop under the skin causing intense irritation.

**manna:** [mana] *v.*, To perplex, befuddle, stump, cause confusion. *De lawya rally manna da man wif hih queshon.* (The lawyer really manna that man with his question.) "The lawyer really perplexed that man with his question."

**man lappa:** [mẽ lapa] *n.*, Slang term for prostitute or unmarried female sexual partner. Conversely, a promiscuous man can be called a *woman lappa.* See **hobojoe**.

**Mano:** [mãno] n., An ethnic group found primarily in Nimba County in east central Liberia, with a small population in Southern Guinea. Population is roughly 190,000. Also called the *Maa*, they speak a Southeast-Mande language and are closely related culturally and linguistically to the Gio (Dan.) Primarily animistic with some Christian presence.

**ma peepo:** [ma pipo] "my people" *n.*, A phrase used to respectfully address a group. *Ma peepo, A coming go na.* (My people, I coming go now.) "Everybody, I'm getting ready to leave."

**manpo:** [mapo] *n.*, Manpo™. Monosodium glutamate. Originally a brand name, it later came to apply generally to all MSG. A common additive for sauces in Liberia. *Wen yu going een de markeh, yu muh buy one mapo fo me, yah?* (When you going in the market, you must buy one mapo for me, you hear?) "When you going in the market, please buy one bag of MSG for me, OK?

**mar:** [ma:] *n.*, Money, cash. Slang. *Ma man, weh my mar?* (My man, where my money?) "Buddy, where's my money?"

**markeh:** [ma:kɛ] "market" *n.*, 1. A place for buying and selling goods, usually under make-shift shelters. *A fini go to de markeh to buy potato greens.* (I finish go to the market to buy potato greens.) "I went to the market to buy potato greens." 2. The goods sold in a small business. *Wen de rebo enta town de women dem tek deh markeh an run.* (When the rebels entered the town the women them take their market and run.) "When the rebels entered the town, the women took the goods they were selling and ran away." 3. To "make market" means to sell. *She teking de bittaball een town to mek markeh wif ih.* (She taking the bitter ball in town to make market with it.) "She's taking the bitterballs in town to sell them." 4. Illegal drugs. Slang. *Dey smoke two type of markeh een de ghetto. Dey smoke heroin an dey smoke coke.* (They smoke two type of market in the ghetto. They smoke heroin and they smoke coke.) "They smoke two types of drugs in the drug houses: heroin and cocaine."

**marking deer:** [ma:kī dija] *n.*, See **mountain deer.**

**mysef:** [masɛf] "myself" *interj.* This word is often heard when one speaker is agreeing with the other. Similar to "me too" in Standard English. E.g. Speaker 1. *A ain wan eat dry rice today.* (I ain't want eat dry rice today.) "I don't want to eat plain rice today. Speaker 2. *Mysef! A na wan dry rice!* (Myself, I not want dry rice!) "I don't want plain rice either."

**ma weeken on yu:** [ma wikḗ õ ju] "my weekend is on you" *idiom.*, A not-so-subtle way to ask for money. This formula can be applied to other events such as Christmas, July 26th (Liberian Independence Day), etc. *Harris, my Christmas on yu.* (Harris, my Christmas on you.) "Harris, I am expecting you to make my holiday a good one (by giving me money)."

**mean:** [mī] 1. *adj.*, To be stingy, selfish. *Da man too mean wif hih cycle.* (That man too mean with his cycle.) "That man is stingy with the use of his bicycle." 2. *v.*, To withhold desired goods from another person. *Yu cyan gii me small rice? Ha yu wan mean me so?"* (You can't give me small rice? How you want mean me so?) "You can't give me any rice? Why do you have to be so stingy with me?"

**mean ih:** [mīn ɪ] "mean it" *v.*, To intend, to do purposely. *Da pekin mean ih to chunk me.* (That pekin mean it to chuck me.) "That boy threw something at me on purpose."

**meat:** [mi] *n.*, A small animal. Liberians often see little value in animals beyond their nutritional value. Thus, most small animals are referred to simply as "meat." This double usage is also common in the indigenous languages. *Yu wan so A muh mine yo meat when yu gone?* (You want so I must mind your meat when you gone?) "Do you want me to take care of your animal while you are away?"

**meat ro:** [mi ɹo] "meat road" *n.*, Game trail. A path used by animals in the forest. *A see de meat ro side de wata.* (I see the meat road side the water.) "I saw a game trail beside the river."

**medicine:** [mɛɹasī] n., 1. Fetishes or rituals associated with witchcraft. Used to gain power or provide protection. Not usually used in reference to western drugs. For this see **druss** and **tableh.** *Da man get bulleh-proof medicine.* (The man got bullet-proof medicine.) "That man has a fetish that protects him from bullets." See **zo, moli, witch.** 2. Agricultural chemicals such as insecticide. *Grasshoppa rally been giving me hard tam. A wan go een town to buy de medicine fo ih.* (Grasshopper really been giving me hard time. I want go in town to buy the medicine for it.)

"I have been having a lot of problems with grasshoppers. I want to go in town to buy insecticide for them."

**meet**: [mit'] *v.*, To find, to come across. Often said of impersonal objects. Example 1: *A meet de donfa una de kishen.* (I meet the donfa under the kitchen.) "I found the duck under the kitchen." *De night meet me een de bush.* (The night meet me in the bush.) "Night fell on me in the forest."

**mek farm**: [mek fa:m] "make farm" *v.*, Encompasses all the steps of preparing land for agriculture, from the initial clearing to planting. See **clean farm, brush farm, boin farm** and **scratch farm**.

**mek ih**: [me kɪ] "make it" *v.*, Used rather than "that's why." *Erik looking too dry. Da wa mek ih da woman say he having AIDS.* (Eric looking too dry. That what make it that woman say he having AIDS.) "Erik is very skinny. That's why that woman said he has AIDS."

**mek ih so**: [me kɪ so] "make it so" *v.*, To do what is necessary. *Mek ih so we all can eat somting na.* (Make it so we all can eat something now.) "Do what it takes so we all can eat something now."

**mek mouf**: [mek' mauf] *v.*, To engage in empty talk or boasting. *James wa meking mouf say he know Ma Ellen.* (James was making mouth say he know Ma Ellen.) "James was boasting without warrant saying he knows Ellen Johnson-Sirleaf."

**melon**: [melõ] *n.*, Watermelon. This is the only commonly available melon in Liberia.

**Mende**: [mẽde] *n.*, A Southwest-Mande speaking people group. A dominant ethnic group of Sierra Leone, they are also found in smaller numbers (approximately 20,000) in western Liberia in Cape Mount county as well as the Vahun district of Lofa county. The Mende and are closely related culturally and linguistically to the Bandi. They practice African traditional religion, Christianity or Islam.

**Merico**: [meɹiko] *n.*, Short-hand for "Americo-Liberians." The descendants of the freed slaves who founded the Republic of Liberia. See also **Congo**.

**Micky Mouse show**: [mɪki maus ʃo] *n.*, May be used for any animated film or cartoon. *De wa showing one Micky Mouse show to de video club las night.* (They were showing one Micky Mouse show to the video club last night.) "They were showing a cartoon at the video club last night." Note: The word **cartoon** in Liberian English refers to a cardboard box.

**mine**: [mãĩ] "mind" *v.*, To care for, to look after. *A sen Fatu to go mine de baby.* (I sent Fatu to go mind the baby.) "I sent Fatu to take care of the baby."

**minero wata**: [mɪnaɪo wata] "mineral water" *n.*, Bottled or factory-produced bagged water. Commonly sold on the street. For sanitary reasons many people prefer drinking water bagged in local factories over water bagged at home.

**missing**: [mɪsĩ] *v.*, Used commonly rather than "to be lost." Even inanimate objects are said to "get missing." For example, *Ma inkpen geh missing.* (My ink pen get missing.) "I lost my pen."

**missy**: [mɪsi] *n.*, A term of respect for adult women

**mo**: [mo] "more" *adj.*, Many, numerous. In contrast the Standard English usage of the world, Liberians do not typically use "more" for statements of comparison. (For this see **plenty, pa** and **den**) *Da man geh mo pineapple to hih farm.* (That man get more pineapple to his farm.) "That man has a lot of pineapples on his farm."

**moda feeling**: [mʌda fiĩ] "mother feeling" *n.*, The feeling of intimacy or emotional closeness between an mother and her child. *Harriet na born da geh, buh she geh real moda feeling fo hur.* (Harriet not born that girl, but she get real mother feeling for her.) "Harriet didn't give birth to that girl, but she feels as close to her as her own daughter."

**MODEL**: [modɛl] *n.*, The Movement for Democracy in Liberia. A rebel faction launched in 2003 from Côte d'Ivoire against Charles Taylor.

**moli**: [mɔri] *adj.*, Pertaining to Islamic sorcery. From the Mandingo word *moli* meaning "priest." *Da ole man been doing hih moli activities an causing mo prorem een town dee few days.* (The old man been doing his moli activities and causing more problem in town these few days.) "That old man has been doing his Islamic sorcery and causing a lot of problems in town recently." See **moliman**.

**moliman**: [mɔrimẽ] *n.*, A marabout or Muslim shaman who uses his knowledge of the Koran and esoteric Arabic texts to cast spells and provide protection and blessing to paying clients. They are known for making **lasmo** and **nesi** and may be sought even by non-Muslims. They may also be called **karmo**, although technically the *karmo* earn their living primarily by teaching the Qur'an while *molimen* support themselves exclusively through their secret arts.

**moneybus**: [mʌni bəs] *n.*, A term occasionally heard in reference to a small bus that is used to transport paying passengers. This word is somewhat dated and today they are more commonly called a **hole-hole** or simply a *bus.*

**money man**: [mʌni mẽ] *n.*, A wealthy person. *Fomba pa da real money man.* (Fomba pa that real money man.) "Fomba's father is a very rich man."

**monger**: [mõngɔ] 1. *n.*, Rumor, gossip. 2. *v.*, To spread gossip

**moni kalama**: [mɔni kalama] *n.*, A watery rice porridge eaten for breakfast. From the Mandingo *mɔni* "rice porridge." *Deh one geh wa can be passing yeh een de moning selling moni kalama.* (There one girl what can be passing here in the morning selling moni kalma.) "There is a girl who comes by here in the morning selling rice porridge."

**monkey apple**: [mɔkɛ apɔ] *n.*, Most commonly, the edible fruit of the *Parinarium macrophyllum* tree which grows wild in the coastal sections of Liberia. This term can also be applied to a variety of other wild edible fruits.

**monkey boid**: [mɔkɛ bwoɪ] "monkey bird" *n.*, The White-crested Hornbill. *Tropicranus albocristatus albocristatus.* A large-billed bird with a white head and dark feathers. Named for its habit of traveling with troops of monkeys, sharing food and alerting them of danger with a loud cry.

**monkey bridge**: [mɔkɛ bɹiʃ] *n.*, A suspension bridge made from lianas used to cross small rivers in the forest. Made by members of the Poro in great secrecy. Uncommon these days, except in isolated regions of the country. *De monkey bridge rope spoiling small small, so dey coming fis ih.* (The monkey bridge rope spoiling small small, so they coming fix it.) "The vines of the monkey bridge are getting ruined little by little, so they are going to fix it."

**monkey checkers**: [mɔkɛ t͡ʃɛkɔs] *n.*, A board game known most commonly in English as "mancala." This game is played on a wooden board with two parallel rows of six hollowed out pits, with a larger pit on each end. Players take the game pieces, called seeds, from the holes and drop them one by one into each consecutive pit.

**monkey fly**: [mɔkɛ flaɪ] *n.*, A horse fly. Similar to the tsetse fly but larger.

**monkey fruit**: [mɔkɛ fɹu] *n.*, See **monkey apple**.

**monkey nut**: [mɔkɛ nʌ] *n.*, The rambutan fruit. *Nephelium lappaceum.* A small red fruit covered in long hairs. Inside the outer rind is a large seed covered in a sweet pulp. A popular snack around the Monrovia area.

**motocar**: [motoka:] "motor car" *n.*, An automobile.

**mouf full**: [mauf fo] *adj.*, To be too much to explain. *He cun tok abou wa he see een de war. Hih mouf wa full.* (He couldn't talk about what he seen in the war. His mouth was full.) "He couldn't talk about what he had seen in the war. It was too overwhelming to talk about."

**mountain**: [maũtɪ] *n.*, There are few true mountains in Liberia, but the northern parts of the country feature many inselbergs and foothills. Liberians generally do not distinguish between these and refer to any sizable hill as a mountain. *Da de mountain deh weh awa ole peepo cu go mek sacrifi.* (That the mountain there where our old people could go make sacrifice.) "That's the mountain where our ancestors used to go make sacrifices."

**mountain deer**: [maũfi dijɛ] *n.*, The Zebra Antelope. *Cephalophus doria.* A small duiker with a light brown coat with black stripes. May also refer to the much larger Bongo. *Tragelaphus euryceros.*

**move**: [mu] *v.*, 1. To remove. *A beg yu, plea move de zinc fron owa de hus.* (I beg you, please move the zinc from on the house.) "Please remove the zinc from the top of the house." 2. To change location or position. Used rather than "get off" or "get out". *Move fron de ro.* (Move from the road.) "Get off the road." 3. To be socially active, to be seen often in public. *De tam we wa to Abidjan me an my fren cu be moving togela.* (The time we were to Abidjan me and my friend can be moving together.) "When we were in Abidjan my friend and I were out and about together."

**move behine**: [mu bihãj] "move behind" *v.*, To leave alone. *Wa happen yu chiren cyan move behine da woman?* (What happen you children can't move behind the woman?) "Why can't you children leave that woman alone?"

**muanmuan**: [muæ̃muæ̃] *n.*, 1. Smelly smoked fish. Prepared by first being soaked in brine and then removed and allowed to spoil slightly before being smoked. 2. By derivation this word can also refer to affairs that are metaphorically "stinky." *A na wan puh my han een dis muanmuan money bisneh.* (I not want put my hand een this muanmuan money business.) "I don't want to have any part in this sketchy financial scheme."

**mud-stick**: [mʌsti] *adj.*, Describes buildings made with the traditional wattle and daub method. *A na geh money to build cement hus so A coming fis de mud-stick own.* (I not get money to build cement house so I coming fix the mud-stick own.) "I don't have the money to build a cement block house so I am going to make a wattle and daub one."

**muh**: [mʌ] "must" *v.*, This modal verb is heard often in Liberian English, with much wider sense than in Standard English. 1. To compel someone to perform a certain action due to a rule or law. *Yu muh na enta da fores.* (You must not enter the forest.) "You must not enter that forest." 2. The most common meaning of the word corresponds to the Standard English "should." *A teh de pekin say he muh bring de radio.* (I tell the pekin say he must bring the radio.) "I told the boy he should bring the radio." 3. Will, would. This word is also frequently heard in requests, which may sound rude to the uninitiated Westerner. In this cases the word has a meaning closer to "will." *Yu muh gii me five dala, yah?* (You must give me five dollar, you hear?) "Will you give me five dollars? OK?" 4. Another sense of the word used in requests corresponds to the Standard English "may" and is also used in making requests. *A muh tek de cycle?* (I must take the cycle?) "May I take the bicycle?"

**muppet:** [mʌpɛ] *n.,* 1. Puppets. 2. Cartoon drawings. 3. Cartoon shows. See also **Micky Mouse show.**

**music box:** [musɪ bas] *n.,* 1. An accordion. Popular before the civil war, these instruments are rare in Liberia today. 2. A harmonica. Occasionally found for sale in Monrovia or local markets.

# N

**na**: [na] "now" *adv.*, Immediately, in the present time. Often redoubled for emphasis. *A coming na na.* (I coming now now.) "I'm coming right now." *Na na* can also be stated *Jus na.* "Just now."

**na**: [ná] "not" *adv.*, An adverb used to negate clauses. Distinguished from "now" by a high tone. *A na wan go deh.* (I not want go there.) "I don't want to go there." See also **ain** and **don**.

**name**: [nem] *n.*, Reputation, economic status. *Adam geh name buh he been acting lek small boy dee few days. (Adam got name but he been acting like small boy these few days.)* "Adam is a man of status, but he has been acting like a nobody recently."

**na easy**: [na isi] "not easy" *adj.*, 1. Used rather than difficult, challenging, hard, etc. *De teacha exam wa na easy o! (The teacher exam was not easy o!)* "The teacher's exam was really hard!" 2. Excessive, ridiculous, ostentatious. *Dis woman bluffing bisneh na easy.* (This woman bluffing business not easy.) "The way this woman loves to show off is ridiculous." 3. Incredible, wonderful, splendid, etc. *De feas wa na easy.* (The feast was not easy.) "The feast was incredible."

**na far**: [na fa:] "not far" *adj.*, In Liberia it is common when asking directions to be told that a destination is "not far." This may mean anything from a few minutes to several hours of travel time.

**nafu**: [nafʊ] "knockfoot" *n.*, A game popular among young girls. Played by clapping and stomping certain rhythms that are passed to a partner to imitate.

**nakeh**: [nɛkɛ] "naked" 1. *v.*, To undress *"Eh pekin, why you nakeh yourself?* (Eh pekin, why you naked yourself?) "Little boy, why did you take your clothes off?" 2. This word can also be used to emphasize the severity of a thing. *De nakeh scent wa coming mek me to vomit.* (The naked scent was coming make me to vomit.) "Just the smell itself was about to make me vomit."

**napleh**: [naplɛ] *n.*, Sailfish. *Istiophorus spp.* Often dried and sold in coastal area markets.

**naval**: [nevɔ] *n.*, Used rather than "belly-button".

**naval string**: [nevɔ stɹĩ] *n.*, Umbilical cord

**neegee**: [nid͡ʒi] *n.*, A dangerous aquatic spirit that is believed to live in rivers. They are said to grab unsuspecting victims and drown them. It is believed that through witchcraft a person can become a neegee and harm their enemies. From the Bassa language.

**nesi**: [nesi] *n.*, A liquid charm made by Muslim clerics. After a passage from the Koran is written on a wooden writing slate called a **wala**, the ink is washed off the board and used for ritual bathing or drinking. *De karmo gii de boy nesi wata. Da wa mek ih he cleva een school.* (The karmo give the boy nesi water. That what make it he clever in school.) "The Muslim cleric gave the boy nesi water. That's why he does so well in school." See **moliman**.

**newa**: [nɛwa] "never" *adv.*, Used to negate sentences, although not with the same sense of finality this word has in Standard English. A closer meaning in Standard English would be "did not." For example, *He newa go een town* (He never go in town.) "He never went in town." This does not mean the man has never before been to town, but rather that he did not go to town during the particular time being referenced.

**Newa-Die-Church**: [nɛwa daɪ t͡ʃɔʃ] "Never-Die-Church" *n.*, An infamous cult started in Liberia in the 1990s. Its members believed that faithful believers would never die. They also believed earthly family relationships were irrelevant and incest was acceptable. It was finally squelched under Charles Taylor's regime.

**newa mine yah**: [nɛwa mãj jæ] "never mind, you hear" *idiom.*, Used to comfort someone who is hurting or sick. Equivalent to Standard English "I'm sorry. Don't worry about it. Everything will be OK," etc. Note: In Liberian English to say that one is sorry is often understood to be taking blame for an incident.

**night gown**: [naɪ gã] *n.*, Casual evening clothes, pajamas. Considered acceptable attire in rural Liberia for hosting visitors or going on a **walk-about**.

**night suit**: [naɪ su] *n.*, See **night gown**.

**niko**: [nɪkɔ] "nickle" *n.*, A five Liberty dollar (LD) note. Slang usage. *Eh ba, yu muh gii me niko to buy kuway.* (Eh ba, you must give me nickle to buy kool-aid.) "Hey friend, please give me five LD to buy a cold drink."

**noda mo**: [nɔda mo] "another more" *adj.*, Another. *We geh noda mo rice bag to de kishin.* (We got another more rice bag to the kitchen.) "We have another bag of rice in the kitchen."

**noko**: [noko] *n.*, A low ranking soldier. Often used in reference to the Frontier Force soldiers of the past. *De noko nyuse to flok peepo when dey refuse to pay de hut tax.* (The soldiers used to flog people when they refused to pay the hut tax.) "The soldiers used to beat people when they refused to pay their hut taxes."

**no play**: [no ple] *adv.*, Seriously, no joke. *A coming bring de mar, no play.* (I coming bring the mar, no play.) "I'm going to bring the money, no joke."

**normal days**: [nomɔ des] *n.*, The normal days of antebellum Liberia. *Nomal days we nyuse to have plenty big big huses yah, buh de war fini spoil all.* (Normal days we used to have plenty big big houses yes, but the war finish spoil all.) "Before the war we used to have a lot of big houses here, but they were all ruined in the war."

**NPFL**: [ɛn pi ɛf ɛl] *n.*, The National Patriot Front of Liberia. A rebel faction led by Charles Taylor which initiated the Liberian civil war. Comprised mainly of soldiers from the Mano and Gio ethnic groups. The NPFL was responsible for many atrocities against the Krahn and Mandingo people.

**nup**: [nʌp] *v.*, To be high on drugs. *De boy smoke markeh. Na he nupping.* (The boy smoke market. Now he nupping.) "The boy smoked drugs and now he is high."

**nyama-nyama**: [ɲamaɲama] 1. *adj.*, Messed up, in a state of disorder. Possibly derived from the Mandingo *nyama* "garbage." *A cyan sleep een dis nyama-nyama room.* (I can't sleep in this nyama-nyama room.) "I can't sleep in this messy room." 2. *adj.*, Miscellaneous, assorted. *A na wan buy all dee nyama-nyama ting dem.* (I not want buy all these nyama-nyama thing them.) "I don't want to buy all these miscellaneous items." 3. *n.*, Miscellaneous items. *A going sell dogafleh an ola nyama-nyama to de markeh.* (I going sell dogafleh and other nyama nyama to the market.) "I am going to sell used clothes and other miscellaneous things at the market."

**nyan**: [ɲã] *adj.*, Naive, foolish, ignorant of local customs. From the Mano language. *De way Mary say da ting, she looking too nyan.* (The way Mary say that thing, she looking too nyan.) "The way Mary said that thing makes her look very naive."

**nyew rice**: [ɲiu ɹaɪs] "new rice" *n.*, Freshly harvested rice. Prized for its taste. Also valuable in ritual sacrifice.

**nyoung boy chief**: [ɲiə̃ boɪ t͡ʃif] "young boy chief" *n.*, The village youth leader. *De nyoung boy chief fini call meeting fo all de yute.* (The young boy chief finish call meeting for all the youth.) "The village youth leader has called a meeting for all the youth."

# O

o (1): [ó] *interj.*, Added at the end of sentences for emphasis. Used liberally in Liberian English. *Da na me o!* (That not me o!) "It certainly wasn't me!"

o (2): [ó] *interj,.* Said with high tone to express surprise or incredulity. *O? Martha na go een town?* (Oh? Martha now go in town?) "Oh? Martha already went to town?"

o (3): [o] 1. *interj.*, Used for emphasis in a narrative when giving a list of different items. *Deh wa plenty animo to de village: chicken o, donfa, goat o.* (There were plenty animal to the village: chicken o, donfa o, goat o.) "There were many animals in the village: chickens, ducks, goats." 2. *conj.*, Whatever, any. *Potato green o, cassava leaf o, palava sauce o, A can fis all.* (Potato green o, cassava leaf o, palaver sauce o, I can fix all.) "Potato greens, cassava leaf, palaver sauce or whatever, I am able to make it." 3. *conj.*, Whether or not. *A gapping o, A na gapping o, de ole ma can still feed me.* (I gapping O, I not gapping O, the old ma can still feed me.) "Whether or not I am hungry, the old lady still feeds me."

Octopus: [ɔtopus] *n.*, A prominent battle of the Liberian civil war in which hundreds of civilians were killed. In the early morning hours of October 15, 1992, Charles Taylor invaded the sleeping city of Monrovia with his NPFL fighters. He gave the attack the code name "Operation Octopus" in reference to the many "tentacles," or bands of rebels, that would strangle the city.

ole ma: [o ma] "old ma" *n.*, A term of respect for older woman. *Deh one ole ma to my yar wa can fis red oil.* (There one old ma to my yard what can fix red oil.) "There is a old lady in my compound who makes red palm oil."

ole man: [o mɛ̃] "old man" *n.*, Term of respect for an elderly man. *Ole man Kollie wa de town secretary.* (Old man Kollie was the town secretary.) "Old man Kollie was the town secretary." See also **papay**.

Ole Man Begga: [o mɛ̃ bega] "Old Man Beggar" *n.*, An informal masquerade put on by children, usually during the Christmas season. One of the children dresses up in a costume with a mask and travels around with friends to collect money. *One ole man begga pas by de hus dih morning wif hih fren dem beating buckeh.* (One old man beggar passed by the house this morning with his friend them beating on bucket.) "A kid came by the house this morning dressed up as Old Man Beggar with his friends beating on buckets like drums."

**Ole Man Musa:** [o mē musa] *n.,* A pejorative term for a **sandcutta** or **moliman** (Muslim shaman.) *De tam malaria kesh yu, yu muh na go to Ole Man Musa to fine oh who de one witch yu!* (The time malaria catch you, you must not go to Old Man Musa to find who the one witch you.) "When you get malaria, you should not go to the Muslim shaman to find out who put a curse on you."

**ole peepo:** [o pipo] "old people" *n.,* Elder, ancestors. *Awa ole peepo meet plenty wile wile animo een dis bush, buh dey fini drive all.* (Our old people meet plenty wild wild animal in this bush, but they finish drive all.) "Our ancestors found lots of wild animals in this forest, but they drove them all away."

**on:** [ã] *prep.,* To be doing, to be engaged in something. *Wa ting yor on na?* (What thing y'all on now?) "What are you all up to now?"

**one:** [wɔ̃] 1. *pro.,* One's self. *Ma one na abo to build dis hus.* (My one not able to build this house.) "I am not able to build this house by myself." 2. *adj.,* A particular one. Occasionally used in place of the indefinite article for emphasis. *Joseph come to de church wif one bright guy* (Joseph come to the church with one bright guy.) "Joseph came to the church with a light skinned man."

**one one:** [wɔ̃wɔ̃] *adv.,* 1. Occasionally, infrequently. *Yu can see monkey one one een dis bush, buh ih ain plenty yah.* (You can see monkey one one in this bush, but it ain't plenty here.) "Occasionally you can see monkeys in this forest, but they aren't common here." *A can yeh Bassa one one.* (I can hear Bassa one one.) "I can understand a few words in Bassa." 2. One by one. This construction can also be used for other numbers. *Yor muh come one one to receive yo pay.* (Y'all must come one one to receive your pay.) "You all should come one by one to receive your pay." 3. One for each. Again, this construction can also be used for higher numerals. *He coming gii uh one one plate.* (He coming give us one one plate.) "He's going to give each of us one plate."

**one tam:** [wɔ̃ tã] *adv.,* 1. Once and for all. *Why na yu jus go pay Jusu one tam?* (Why not you just go pay Jusu one time.) "Why don't you just go pay Jusu once and for all." 2. This may also be used to express exasperation, similar to the informal Standard English usage of "already." *Yu cyan dress one tam?* (You can't dress one time?) "Can't you move over already?" 3. At once, suddenly. *De tam he see de lepor he jump one tam.* (The time he see the leopard he jump one time.) "When he saw the leopard he jumped suddenly."

**oping mo:** [opĩ mo] "open mole" *n.,* 1. A babies' fontanel. *Ma baby oping mole swella.* (My baby open mole swollen.) "My babies fontanel is swollen." 2. A folk medical condition believed by Liberians to be caused by

122

the reopening of the fontanel in adults. Characterized by severe headaches. *A suffering fron open mole dee few days.* (I suffering from open mole these few days.) "I've been having serious headaches recently."

**opium:** [opjɔ̃] *n.,* A local name for marijuana. *Doh gronna boys can smoke too mush oh opium.* (Those gronna boys can smoke too much of opium.) "Those gangsters smoke a lot of marijuana."

**opossum:** [opasɔ̃] *n.,* The African Giant Pouched Rat. *Cricetomys gambianus.* A large rodent common in Liberia. Prized for bush-meat. *A kesh one big opossum de tam A wa brushing my farm.* (I catch one big opossum the time I was brushing my farm.) "I caught a big pouched rat when I was clearing my farm."

**orosonjo:** [oɹosõd͡ʒo] *n.,* A political opportunist. One who values money and power more than justice and integrity.

**outside chile:** [ausaɪ t͡ʃaɪl] "outside child" *n.,* A child born out of wedlock. *Ma wife born me tdee chiren, an A geh one outside chile.* (My wife born me three children, and I get one outside child.) "I had three children with my wife, and one illegitimate child."

**owa:** [owa] "over" *prep.,* On, on top of. *De chicken dem can sleep over de hus wen nighttam com.* (The chicken them can sleep over the house when nighttime come.) "The chickens sleep on top of the house at night."

**own:** [oũ] *pro.* Used to specify one out of a group. *Gii me de five dala own.* (Give me the five dollar own.) "Give me the one for five dollars."

**owna:** [oũna] "own of" *adj., pro.,* A possessive pronoun. *Hih owna fren dem een school na.* (His own friend them in school now.) "His friends are in school now."

# P

**pa** (1): [pa] *n*, Father. *Hih pa da tall man stanning so.* (His pa that tall man standing so.) "His father is that tall man standing over there.)

**pa** (2): [pa] "part" *n.*, On one's part, as for. *He pa, hih rice fini.* (He part, his rice finish.) "As for him, his rice is gone."

**pa** (3): [pa] "past" *adv.*, Used in statements of comparison. *Da pekin tall pa hih big brola.* (That pekin tall past his big brother.) "That kid is taller than his older brother."

**packing**: [pakī] *n.*, Packing station. A place where cars and buses are loaded for departure to various locations. *She fini go to de packing to fine car.* (She finish go to the packing to find car.) "She already left for the packing station to find a car."

**packuh**: [pækʌ] "pack up" v., Used rather than packed, piled, jammed together, etc. *De tam de war wa going on, plenty peepo packuh eenside Doe stadium.* (The time the war was going on, plenty people pack up inside Doe stadium.) "While the war was going on, many people were jammed together in the Samuel K. Doe stadium."

**pain tableh**: [pī tablɛ] *n.*, Used rather than pain reliever, aspirin, etc. *Ma ho body hiting, so A will go buy pain tableh.* (My whole body hurting, so I will go buy pain tablet.) "My whole body is hurting, so I will go buy some pain reliever."

**papa**: [papa] *n.*, Used in directly addressing one's father or other authority figure. *Papa, yu can plea credih me small somting?* (Papa, you can please credit me small something?) "Dad, can you please lend me a little money?"

**pap-pap**: [papap] *n.*, A colloquial term for flip-flops. More commonly called **slipper**.

**palava**: [palawa] "palaver" *n.*, 1. An argument, disagreement. *Dey go to de station to tok de palava.* (They go to the station to talk the palaver.) "They went to the police station to discuss the case." 2. A problem, issue. *Hih woman palava mek ih so he cun sleep las night.* (His woman palaver make it so he couldn't sleep last night.) His problem with that woman made it so he couldn't sleep last night." 3. Matters pertaining to (Basilectal usage.) *Da tam we na know curren palava.* (That time we not know current palaver.) "At that time we didn't know about electricity." See also **bisneh**.

**palava hut**: [palawa hɔ] "palaver hut" *n.*, An open sided round building traditionally used as a place to settle disputes. *De chief dem leshuring una* *de palava hut.* (The chief them lecturing under the palaver hut.) "The chief and the others are talking under the palaver hut."

**palava sauce**: [palawa saus] *n.,* A slimy sauce made from jute leaves. *Corchorus olitorius.* Served over rice.

**palm**: [pã] *n,* This word is almost exclusively used in reference to the oil palm. *Elaeis guineensis.* Other species of palm have their own name like *coconut* and **bamboo.**

**palm boid**: [pã bwoɪ] "Palm Bird" *n.,* Hornbill. Medium sized birds with large bills. Common species in Liberia include the Allied Hornbill, *Lophoceros semitasciatus* and the Yellow-casqued Hornbill, *Ceratogymna elata.* These species feed on palm nuts and other forest fruits.

**palm butta**: [pã bʌta] "palm butter" *n.,* A thick, brownish-red gravy made from the nuts of the oil palm. Commonly made with beef or seafood and served over rice. Indigenous to southeastern Liberia. *Me pa, A enjoy palm butta den all de ola soup dem.* (Me part, I enjoy palm butter than all the other soup them.) "As for me, I like palm butter better than any other sauce."

**palm cabbage**: [pã kabɛʒ] *n.,* The edible white inner head of an oil or raffia palm. Harvesting it destroys the tree. The taste resembles cabbage, but since most Liberians consider it to be a **hungry food,** it is rarely eaten today. *A sen Junior to cut some palm cabbage.* (I sent Junior to cut some palm cabbage.) "I sent Junior to cut some palm cabbage."

**palm kana**: [pã kana] "palm kernel" *n.,* The inner kernel of the oil palm nut. Used to make palm oil or for recreational snacking. *A meh doh pekin dem bussing palm kana una de plum tree.* (I met those pekin them busting palm kernels under the plum tree.) "I found those boys breaking open palm kernels under the mango tree."

**palm kana oil**: [pã kana ɔj] *n,* A clear oil made from the kernels of oil palm nuts. Used for cooking. Also commonly used as a "poor man's" skin moisterizer. *We coming tek dis palm kana an mek ih wif palm kana oil.* (We coming take this palm kernel and make it with palm kernel oil.) "We are going to take these palm kernels and make oil out of them."

**palm wine**: [pã wãj] *n.,* An extremely potent alcoholic beverage made from the sap of the oil or raffia palm. (*Wen hus dauping tam reesh, peepo can drink too mush oh palm wine.* (When house daubing time reach, people can drink too much of palm wine.) "When it comes time to daub houses, people drink a lot of palm wine."

**pamfleh**: [pamflɛ] "pamphlet" *n.,* Used rather than magazine, brochure, booklet, etc.

**pan-pan**: [pǽpǽ] *n.*, A motor scooter. The word is an ideophone of the sound of the horn. *Pan-pan cyan run lek motobike.* (Pan-pan can't run like motorbike.) "A motor scooter is not as a fast as a motorbike."

**papay**: [pape] *n.*, An old man. *Yeh de play weh all doh papay dem cu be leshuring.* (Here the place where all those papays them can be lecturing.) "Here's the place where all the old men used to chat."

**papu**: [papu] *n.*, Thatch tiles woven from the leaves of the raffia palm. The most common form of roofing in rural Liberia. From the Krahn language. *Papu cyan staylohn. By ness year A will be fising nyew one.* (Papu can't stay long. By next year I will be fixing new one.) "Thatch roofing tiles don't last. By next year I will have to make new ones."

**parabo**: [pæɹabo] "parable" *n.*, A proverb. Proverbs are highly valued in traditional Liberian culture as a means of expressing values indirectly. *We de Kpelle peepo geh one parabo say, 'Ans bear show lepor hih belly.'* (We the Kpelle people got one parable say, 'Ants bear show leopard his belly.') "We the Kpelle people have a proverb that says, 'Pangolin showed leopard his belly.'"

**paramount chief**: [paɹamaũ t͡ʃifdɔ̄] *n.*, The highest level of tribal authority recognized by the Liberian government. Oversees a network of town and clan chiefs. See **clan** and **chiefdom**.

**pass**: [pa] *v.*, 1. To go by. *My fren coming pass to de hus tomorrow.* (My friend coming pass to the house tomorrow.) "My friend is going to come by the house tomorrow." 2. To move, walk. *Ain yu see ha de chiren dem jus passing all roun on de street dis tam?* (Ain't you see how the children them just passing all round on the street this time?) "Don't you see how the kids are just aimlessly wandering the streets now?"

**passava**: [pasawa] "piassava" *n.*, Another name for the raffia palm. See also **bamboo**.

**passava rice**: [pasawa ɹais] *n.*, Swamp rice. So named because this variety of rice is planted in swamps where raffia palms also grow.

**pass wata**: [pas wata] "pass water" *v.*, To urinate. In Liberia it is not considered indelicate to indicate bodily needs. *Driva plea stop. A wan pass wata.* (Driver please stop. I want pass water.) "Driver please stop. I need to urinate."

**patapata**: [patapata] *n.*, Mud, usually on a road. Possibly from Yoruba *petepete* "soggy, muddy." *De patapata really grap de car ba way o!* (The patapata really grab the car bad way o!) "The car is really stuck in the mud!"

127

**pawpaw**: [pɔpɔ] *n.*, The papaya fruit. *Carica papaya.* A very common plant in Liberia, often found growing on dump sites. Because it is so abundant, the fruit has little market value, especially in rural areas.

**pay car**: [pe ka:] "pay car" *v.*, To charter a vehicle. *I fini pay car to go Buchanan.* (I finish pay car to go Buchanan.) "I have chartered a car to take me to Buchanan."

**pay debt**: [pe detˀ] *v.*, To get even, carry out revenge. (*Da man tink he can insult me so? I will surely pay debt to heen.*) "The man think he can insult me so? I will surely pay debt to him.) "That man thinks he can get away with insulting me? I will surely get my revenge on him."

**peepee**: [pipi] 1. *v.*, To urinate. *Liberian man ain shame to stan side de ro to peepee.* (Liberian man ain't shame to stand side the road to peepee.) "Liberian men are not ashamed to urinate standing by the road." See **pass wata.** 2. *n.*, Urine.

**peepo**: [pipo] "people" *n.*, 1. One's relations, family. *Ma peepo dem to de hus.* (My people them to the house.) "My family is at the house." 2. An indirect way of expressing one's opinion. *People ain wan to be eating so so breh.* (People ain't want to be eating so so bread.) "People, myself included, don't want to be eating only bread."

**pekin**: [pikĩ] *n.*, A young boy. From the Portuguese *pequenino. Pekin, wa happing yu crying so?* (Pekin, what happening you crying so?) "Little boy, why are you crying like that?"

**pele**: [pele] *n.*, A girl's stomping and clapping game similar to **nafu.**

**pensil**: [pɛ̃sɪ] *n.*, Mortar pestle. *Ma Lurpu say hur pensil spoil, so A coming go een de bush to cut stick so A can fis nyew one fo hur.* (Ma Lurpu say her pensil spoil, so I coming go in the bush to cut stick so I can fix new one for her.) "Ma Lurpu said her pestle was broken, so I'm going to go in the forest to cut a stick so I can make a new one for her."

**penten**: [pɛ̃tɛ̃] *n.*, A small species of silvery ocean fish. A valued food item.

**peppa**: [pɛpa] "Pepper" *n.*, Hot pepper, *Capsicum frutenscens.* Besides being an ubiquitous part of Liberian sauces served over rice, hot pepper is also used to discipline unruly children. *De radio man say we muh na puh peppa een de chiren eye to punish dem.* (The radio man say we must not put pepper in the children eye to punish them.) "The man on the radio said we should not put pepper in children's eyes to discipline them."

**peppa boid**: [pɛpa bɔɪ] "pepper bird" *n.*,. The Common Bulbul. *Pycnonotus barbatus inornatus.* This thrush-like, drab colored bird is the national bird of Liberia.

**peppa bush**: [pɛpa buɪʃ] "pepper bush" *n.*, A colloquialism meaning "a means of extra income." *Peter buy da taxi to be hih lil peppa bush.* (Peter buy that taxi to be his little pepper bush.) "Peter bought that taxi to bring in some extra money."

**peppa soup**: [pɛpa sup] "pepper soup" *n.*, An extremely spicy broth made from fresh hot peppers and served over rice. Especially popular in southeast Liberia. *A geh fresh co, buh A drin some peppa soup an A feeling betta small.* (I get fresh cold, but I drink some pepper soup and I feeling better small.) "I have a cold, but I drank some pepper soup and I am feeling a little better."

**piazza**: [piæsa] *n.*, Used rather than porch, veranda, etc. *De bossman say he wan puh screen to de piazza.* (The bossman say he want put screen to the piazza.) "The boss said he wants to screen in the porch."

**pick**: [pikʼ] *v.*, Used rather than choose, select, appoint, etc. *De presiden pick some of de big big man dem to be hur adviso.* (The president pick some of the big big man them to be her advisor.) "The president chose some of the important men to be her advisors."

**pick fuss**: [pi fʌs] *v.* Used rather than nag, pester, etc. *Hoday my woman can be picking fuss wif me say my clo ditey.* (Whole day my woman can be picking fuss with me say my clothes dirty.) "My wife is always nagging me saying my clothes are dirty."

**piece of job**: [pis ə jʌb] *n.*, A little work, a small contract. *A geh lil piece of job to do een Gardnersville. A will come back dis eveling.* (I get little piece of job to do in Gardnersville. I will come back this evening.) "I have a small contract in Gardnersville. I will come back this evening."

**pissy**: [pɪsi] *adj.*, Drunk. Slang usage. *Soon ah payday come Dolo will be to de club getting pissy.* (Soon as payday come Dolo will be to the club getting pissy.) "As soon as payday is here Dolo will go to the club and get drunk."

**pitanga**: [pɪtaŋga] *n.*, The Surinam Cherry. *Eugenia uniflora.* A small cultivated tree or shrub with tart, red berries.

**plah**: [pla] "plait" *v.*, To braid. In rural Liberia it is considered improper for a woman to go around with loose, unplaited hair. *A going to Kou so she can plah my hair.* (I going to Kou so she can plait my hair.) "I am going to Kou so she can plait my hair."

**plank**: [plĕkʼ] *n.*, Used rather than board, timber, etc. *A coming carry de powasaw een de bush to cut plank.* (I coming carry the power saw in the bush to cut plank.) "I will take the chainsaw in the forest to cut some boards."

**plank fish**: [plē fiʃ] "plank fish" *n.*, The knifefish. There are two species in Liberia: the large *Papyrocranus afer* and the smaller *Xenomystus nigri.* Both are commonly found in slow moving creeks and rivers. *A wa coming kesh one big plank fish, buh de catguh cut.* (I was coming catch one big plank fish, but the catgut cut.) "I was about to catch a big knifefish, but the fishing line broke."

**plastic**: [plastɪ] *n.*, A plastic bag. *Yu geh plastic fo me to carry dis ting?* (You get plastic for me to carry this thing?) "Do you have a plastic bag I can use to carry this?"

**play** (1): [ple] *n.*, Traditional village festivities which take place around life-cycle events and involve eating, drinking and dancing.

**play** (2): [ple] *v.*, To engage in, to carry out. *Peewee play fun on da geh.* (Peewee play fun on the girl.) "Peewee played a joke on that girl."

**playtoy**: [pletoɪ] *n.*, A child's toy. *Ma chiren dem ain geh plenty playtoy.* (My children them ain't get plenty playtoy.) "My children do not have a lot of toys."

**play sassywood**: [ple sasiwu] *v.*, To administer poison in a trial by ordeal. See **sassywood**.

**plenty**: [plēni] *adj.*, 1. Used rather than many, numerous, lots, etc. *Dey geh plenty snekfish to da wata.* (They got plenty snakefish to that water.) "There are lots of snakefish in that river." 2. "Plenty" can be used in statements of comparison. *Ma Bintu geh plenty chicken den Ma Hawa.* (Ma Bintu got plenty chicken then Ma Hawa.) "Ma Bintu has more chickens than Ma Hawa." 2. Excessive. *De work plenty fo uh to do today.* (The work plenty for us to do today.) "There is too much work for us to do today."

**plum**: [plɔ] *n.*, A mango. *Mangifera indica. Ma owna plum tree cyan bear again.* (My own plum tree can't bear again.) "My own mango tree doesn't produce fruit anymore."

**policeman**: [polis mē] *n.*, Colloquial term for the gray duiker. They are the first animals to come when a hunter imitates their distress call, like a policeman comes when they hear a disturbance. More commonly called **fooly tongor**.

**pogy**: [pogi] *n.*, The Atlantic Menhaden. *Brevoortia tyrannus.* A marine fish similar to a herring. Commercially valuable.

**poopoo**: [pupu] 1. *v.*, To defecate. *A wan poopoo, but de camo door lock.* (I want poopoo, but the commode door lock.) "I need to defecate, but the latrine door is locked." 2. *n.*, feces.

**Poor Joe:** [poʤo] *n.,* A type of small, common ocean fish. Edible, but relatively undesirable. See also **gbapleh.**

**popoh:** [popo] *n.,* A small ethnic group who live in settlements along the Liberian coast. Originally from Togo and Benin. Most work as fishingmen, using beach seine nets.

**porkay:** [pɔke] *n.,* A large amount of money. Slang usage.

**Poro:** [pɔrɔ] *n.,* A secretive fraternal initiation society. Present in most ethnic groups in Western and Central Liberia, as well as the forest regions of Guinea and Sierra Leone. This society controls many day to day aspects of life for rural Liberians. Initiation is considered compulsory for boys when they reach adolescence. See **Sande, bush school, devil** and **zo.**

**potato:** [poteto] *n.,* Used in reference to local sweet potato varieties. For imported potatoes see **Irish potato.**

**potato greens:** [poteto gɹĩs] n., Sweet potato leaves. Used to make the most common sauce in Liberia.

**potta:** "potter" *n.,* A white clay used in rituals and occasionally eaten. Also called **country chalk.**

**powa:** [pawa] "power" *n.,* 1. Energy, strength. *Breh cyan gii me powa lek rice.* (Bread can't give me power like rice.) "Bread doesn't give me energy like rice." 2. Authority. *De presiden geh powa owa de whole country.* (The president got power over the whole country.) "The president has authority over the whole country."

**pregnant:** [pɹɛnɛ] *v.,* To impregnate. *Paye de man wa pregnant de geh.* (Paye the man what pregnant the girl.) "Paye is the one who got that girl pregnant." For the Standard English adjective "pregnant," see **belly.**

**present:** [pɹɛsẽ] v., To give a gift. *De tam yu come fron Monrovia wa ting yu will present me?* (The time you come from Monrovia what thing you will present me?) "When you come back from Monrovia what gift are you going to bring for me?"

**press:** [pɹɛs] v., Used rather than "iron" in reference to clothes. *Roberts say he muh press hih suit befo he can go to church.* (Roberts say he must press his suit before he can go to church.) "Roberts said he had to iron his suit before he could go to church."

**pressure:** [pɹɛʃʌ] *n.,* Refers to blood pressure. *Enoch say he suffring fron pressure.* (Enoch say he suffering from pressure.) "Enoch said he is struggling with high blood pressure."

**prophet church:** [pɹafɛ ʧoʃ] *n.,* A Pentecostal church, often led by a charismatic preacher who is believed to possess great spiritual power.

**prorem**: [pɹaɹẽ] "problem" *n.*, Used rather than issues, concerns, etc. *Da man ain geh prorem. We muh go aks heen.* (The man ain't got problem. We must go ask him.) "That man doesn't have any issues (and is trustworthy). We should go ask him."

**pull**: [po] *v.*, To get along, to understand one another. *Da wa mek ih dog an monkey cyan pull.* (That what make it dog and monkey can't pull.) "That's why dogs and monkeys don't get along."

**pull swear**: [po suɛ] *v.*, To take back a curse.

**pull witch**: [po wiʃ] *v.*, To exorcise an evil spirit. *De tam John fall off dey call one kpangba man to pull witch on heen.* (The time John fall off they call one kpangba man to pull witch on him.) "When John went crazy they called a witch doctor to remove the evil spirit from him." See **witch**.

**pump** (1): [pɔmp] *n.*, Used rather than faucet, spigot, etc. Most commonly heard in reference to water wells with machine pumps.

**pump** (2): [pɔmp] *v.*, To ask repeatedly. *Ma peepo can be pumping me say 'Wa tam yu coming marry?'* (My people can be pumping me say, 'What time you coming marry?') "My family is always asking me, 'When are you going to marry?"

**punking**: [pʌ̃kĩ] "pumpkin" *n.*, Butternut squash. A common folk belief in Liberia is that a small notch must be made in a pumpkin before it is loaded into a car. Failure to do so is considered very risky and may result in the car having a serious accident. *Yu muh mark de punking befo yu puh ih een de car.* (You must mark the pumpkin before you put in the car.) "You need to make a small cut in the pumpkin before you put it in the car."

**push-push**: [puʃpuʃ] *n.*, A home-made, hand-pushed cart used to transport heavy materials.

**put mouf on**: [pʊ mɔf ã] "put mouth on" *idiom.*, 1. To give one's opinion, input. *De tam we meking palava, eryone can put mouf on ih.* (The time we making palaver, everyone can put mouth on it.) "When we are having an argument, everyone has to put in their two cents." 2. To gossip. *Yor muh na put mouf on me wen A move fron yeh.* (Y'all must not put mouth on me when I move from here.) "You should not gossip about me when I leave."

**pwipe**: [pwaɪp] *n.*, Any cylinderical tube. Used rather than "drain." *De rat fall don de pwipe.* (The rat fall down the pipe.) "The mouse fell down the drain."

**pwipefish**: [pwaɪp fɪʃ] "pipefish" *n.*, Can refer to several varieties of elongated, predatory ocean fish such as barracuda.

# Q

**quick**: [kwɪkˀ] *adv.*, Used more often than "fast" and often redoubled for emphasis. *Go quick quick an buy de rubba so we can go.* (Go quick quick and buy the rubber so we can go.) "Hurry up and buy the rubber so we can go."

# R

**rabbit**: [ɹabɪ] *n.*, The Pygmy Antelope. *Neotragus pygmasus.* A tiny reclusive duiker with a brown coat and white tail. The "rabbit" is a common protagonist in Liberian folktales. Also called **tricky jack.**

**raccoon**: [ɹakũ] *n* This word may be used to refer to a variety of small to medium sized viverrids including civets, genets, linsangs and palm civets. Most common is the African civet, *Civettictis civetta,* which is a medium sized carnivore resembling a cross between a dog and an American raccoon. *Raccoon fini steal my chicken.* (Raccoon finish steal my chicken.) "A civet has taken my chicken."

**rainy season**: [ɹeni sisõ] *n.*, The annual period of heavy precipitation. Rain generally slowly increases from February to July with the wettest months being August and September, after which it slowly tapers off into the dry season.

**raise** (1): [ɹeɪs] *v.*, To keep under one's care. Often said in reference to animals. *A wan fine du baby so A can be raising ih.* (I want find du baby so I can be raising it.) "I want to find a baby mongoose and keep it as a pet."

**raise** (2): [ɹeɪs] *v.*, To lead in singing. *Sis Betty, yu can plee raise one song fo uh?* (Sis Betty, you can please raise one song for us?) "Sister Betty, please lead us in a song."

**ra-ra**: [ɹaɹa] *interj.*, Used in south-eastern Liberia rather than **boc-boc** to announce one's presence at the door.

**rassing up**: [ɹasĩ ə] *v.*, To engage in rowdy physical behavior. *Da pekin love too mush oh rassing up.* (That pekin love too much of rassing up.) "That kid loves being rowdy."

**rat**: [ɹætˀ] *n.*, A general term for small rodents, including mice. *De chiren kesh one bush rat een de trap. Na dey coming roas ih.* (The children catch one bush rat in the trap. Now they coming roast it.) "The children caught a bush rat in their trap. Now they are going to roast it.

**red**: [ɹɛ] 1. *n.,* Used in reference to range of colors from orange to purple. 2. *adj.* Refers to a person with a lighter brown complexion of skin. See also **tomato color**.

**red ans**: [ɹɛ æs] "red ants" *n.,* Red Weaver Ants. *Oecophylla smaragdina.* These large ants often form colonies on fruit trees, weaving nests of leaves together from the silk of the pupae.

**red deer**: [ɹɛ diɛ] *n,* The Bushbuck. *Tragelaphus scriptus scriptus.* A large antelope that has a red coat with white markings. Males have prominent spiraled horns. Prized for bush-meat.

**red-heh lizay**: [ɹɛ hɛ leze] "red-head lizard" *n., Agama agama.* A common lizard in urban areas. Females are drab brown while males are blue with distinctive red heads.

**red oil**: [ɹɛ ɔj] *n,.* The rich oil made from the exterior pulp of oil palm nuts. It is the most common oil in Liberian cooking. See **palm butta, palm kana oil, boin palm oil** and **torbagee oil**.

**red rice**: [ɹɛ ɹaɪs] *n.,* Rice that is cooked and mixed with red oil. Used in ceremonies and ritual sacrifices to ancestral or forest spirits.

**reduce**: [ɹidus] *v.,* To lose weight. Unless one is morbidly obese, this is generally not considered desirable in Liberia. *Ma man, yu rally reduce!* (My man, you really reduce!) "Buddy, you've really lost a lot of weight."

**reed**: [ɹid] *n.,* True bamboo. *Bambusa spp.* The term **bamboo** in Liberian English refers to the raffia palm. *A going een de bush to cut reed.* (I going in the bush to cut reed.) "I'm going in the forest to cut some bamboo."

**reesh**: [ɹiʃ] "reach" *v.,* 1. To go to another location. *Wen A fini working A will reesh to de hus.* (When I finish working I will reach to the house.) "When I'm done working I will go to the house." A common parting phrase is. *OK, A reeshing.* (OK, I reaching.) "OK, I'm leaving now." 2. To arrive. *A reesh een town las night.* (I reach in town last night.) "I arrived in town last night." 3. To pass a decision on a matter to another person. *De palava reesh to yu.* (The palaver reach to you.) "The matter is in your hands."

**report**: [ɹipɔt'] *v.,* To tell on, rat out, tattle, expose. In Liberian culture it is considered extremely improper to compromise another person's means of income by reporting their unscrupulous activities to a higher authority. *De bossman sack Zazay afta Ezra report hih chopping bisneh.* (The bossman sack Zazay after Ezra report his chopping business.) "The bossman fired Zazay after Ezra exposed his corrupt activities."

**resembo**: [ɹisɛmbɔ] "resemble" *v.*, Used rather than "looks like." *Doh pekin dem resembo ba way!* (Those pekin them resemble bad way!) "Those boys look so much alike!"

**respect**: [ɹispɛt'] *n.*, A gift used to show deference to another. *Wen de stranga enta de town, he meet de town chief an gii respect to heen.* (When the stranger enter the town, he meet the town chief and give respect to him.) "When the visitor entered the town, he met the town chief and gave him a gift (showing his respect)."

**rice boid**: [ɹaɪs bɔɪ] "rice bird" *n.*, The African village Weaver. *Textor cucullatus.* A very common bird that lives in large colonies in village trees. They weave basket-like nests from strips of palm leaves, leaving any palm tree in the vicinity of their colony nearly bare. These small birds are extremely fond of rice and cause significant decreases in the annual rice harvest. Farmers often attempt to scare them away with scarecrows and, more recently, strips of shiny metallic tape.

**rice cruss**: [ɹaɪs krʌs] *n.*, See **cruss**.

**rice dust**: [ɹaɪs dʌs] *n.*, See **country breh**.

**rice kishen**: [ɹaɪs kiʃĩ] "rice kitchen" *n.*, A storehouse for rice. The rice is kept in the attic while the ground level is used as a cooking area.

**right by**: [ɹaɪ baɪ] *adj.*, Used rather than next to, close to, etc. *Da co bo shop right by de markeh.* (That cold bowl shop right by the market.) "That cook shop is right by the market." See also **si**.

**ring**: [ɹĩ] *v.*, To play a stringed instrument. *Yu can ring guita?* (You can ring guitar?) "Can you play the guitar?"

**rising**: [ɹaɪsĩ] *n.*, A boil. *Junior geh one hellava rising on hih foot.* (Junior got one hell of a rising on his foot.) "Junior has a huge boil on his leg."

**ro**: [ɹo] "road" *n.*, Any route of transportation, from a footpath to motor road. Usually modified for clarification. *Car ro* "car road" is that which vehicles travel on. *Bush ro* "bush road" is a foot path in the forest. *He walking on de bush ro coming.* (He walking on the bush road coming.) "He is on his way here, walking along the jungle path." See also **co tar**.

**rock**: [ɹak'] *v.*, 1. To knock. *A rock de door buh no one cun answa.* (I rock the door but no one could answer.) "I knocked the door but no one answered." 2. To shake part of one's body. *De music wa hot an all de women dem start rocking deh bunga.* (The music was hot and all the women them start rocking their bunga.) "The music was full of energy and all the women started shaking their rears."

**rock heh:** [ɹak˺ hɛ] "rock head" *n.,* Refers to various species of Drum. A marine, commercially important fish. Named for the bony otoliths found in their heads.

**rogue:** [ɹog] 1. *n.,* Used rather than burglar, thief, etc. In Liberia if someone catches a thief in action, he will often yell, "Rogue, rogue!" causing bystanders to chase after the thief. If the police do not arrive quickly, mob justice may be carried out. *Dey kesh one rogue to Red Light las night.* (They catch one rogue to Red Light last night.) "They caught a thief in Red Light last night." See also **arm robba.** 2. *v.,* To steal. Nonstandard usage. *Hih fren rogue de ole ma.* (His friend rogue the old ma.) "His friend stole from the old woman."

**rogue bar:** [ɹog ba:] "rogue bar" *n.,* Metal grills put over windows to stop thieves from entering a house. Often designed in decorative patterns. *De welda coming fis rogue bar for my window.* (The welder coming fix rogue bar for my window.) "The welder is going to fix security bars for my windows."

**rooduh:** [ɹudʌ] "root-up" *v.,* To dig up a plant by its roots. Used rather than "uproot." *Saye say she coming rooduh all de cassava an mek eddoe garden.* (Saye say she coming root up all the cassava and make eddo garden.) "Saye said she is going to uproot all the cassava and make an eddo garden."

**rope:** [ɹop] *n.,* A general term for any type of cord, from twine to nylon to hemp rope or even vines. See also **country rope.**

**rottin:** [ɹafi] "rotten" *adj.,* Old, rusty, falling apart. *Dis yo rottin car yeh ain correc.* (This your rotten car here ain't correct.) "Your old junker is no good."

**rotting:** [ɹafi] *v.,* To spoil. *Doh pawpaw coming rotting.* (Those pawpaw coming rotten.) "Those papayas are going to spoil."

**ru:** [ɹu] "rude" *n.,* Unruly, incorrigible. Considered a strong epithet in Liberia. *Hoday da ru woman can be putting mouf on peepo.* (Whole day that rude woman can be putting mouth on people.) "That unruly woman is always gossiping about people."

**rubba draw:** [ɹʌbɔ dɹa] "rubber drawers" *n.,* Refers to a variety of items used for incontinence, including rubber pants, and plastic sheets sold for use as a waterproof cover fro diapers.

**rubba disease:** [ɹʌbɔ disis] "rubber disease" *n.,* A type of beetle grub that destroys rubber trees. Similar to **bamboo wolum,** they are occasionally eaten by rubber-farm workers.

**rubba gun**: [ɹʌbɔ gã] "rubber gun" *n.*, A slingshot. *He kill monkey wif rubber gun.* (He kill monkey with rubber gun.) "He killed a monkey with a slingshot."

**run** (1): [ɹã] *v.*, To cause diarrhea. *Da torbagee rally run hih stomach.* (That torbagee really run his stomach.) "That torbagee really gave him diarrhea."

**run** (2): [ɹã] *v.*, To drive quickly. *De driva wa running wif heavy speed!* (The driver was running with heavy speed!) "The driver was going extremely fast!"

**run behind**: [ɹã bihãj] *v.*, To give your attention or energy to something. *Mulabah running behind God bisneh na. He ain get time for all do ole ole ting dem agin.* (Mulabah running behind God business now. He ain't got time for all those old old thing them again.) "Mulabah is trying to follow God's way now. He doesn't pay attention to those old things anymore."

**running stomach**: ɹʌnĩ stəma] *n.*, Diarrhea. *Dih runny stomach bisneh rally giving peepo hard tam dee few days.* (This runny stomach business really giving people hard time these few days.) "Diarrhea has been giving a lot of people problems recently."

**rup**: [ɹʌp] "rub" *v.*, To smooth, to polish. *Wen dey fini daub de hus, da de tam dey coming rup ih fine.* (When they finish daub the house, that the time they coming rub it fine.) "After they finishing daubing the house (with mud), they are going to rub it smooth (with clay.)

# S

**sabi:** [sabi] *adj.,* 1. Cunning, sly, crafty. See **katakata**. 2. Stingy. *Da sabi man cyan buy five dala kuway for hih chiren sef.* (That sabi man cannot buy five dollar Kool-Aid for his children self.) "That stingy man can't even buy five dollars worth of cold drinks for his kids."

**sabu:** [sabu] *n.,* A clean-shaven head. *A reeshing to de barbing saloon. A wan so dey muh cut sabu.* (I reaching to the barbing salon. I want so they must cut sabu.) "I'm going to the barber's booth. I want them to give me a clean shave."

**sack:** [sæk˺] *v.,* To dismiss from a job. Used rather than "fire." *De bossman sack Yakpawolo de tam he fine ouh say he been stealing de cemen.* (The bossman sack Yakpawolo the time he find out say he been stealing the cement.) "The boss fired Yakpawolo when he found out that he had been stealing the cement."

**saka:** [saka] *adj.,* Crazy, out of one's mind. *Yu wan credit fron de bossman agin? Yu saka!* (You want credit from the bossman again? You saka!) "You want to borrow money from the boss again? You are crazy!"

**salad:** [salɛ] *n.,* Potato or egg salad. Commonly served at formal occasions such as weddings and graduations. Lettuce salads are almost unknown in Liberia, except in foreign restaurants.

**same ma, same pa:** [sẽ ma sẽ pa] *idiom.,* A sibling who shares both parents. An important distinction in Liberia where polygamy and cohabitation are commonly practiced. *Peter my broda –same ma, same pa.* (Peter my brother –same ma, same pa.) "Peter is my full brother."

**sancutta:** [sǽkʌta] "sandcutter" *n.,* A traditional diviner who uses sand in his rituals. Through either automatic writing in the sand or throwing cowry shells and interpreting the patterns, the sandcutter is believed to be able to predict the future or determine guilt. *A wen to one sandcutta wa tell me say da my Aunt Hawa wa witch me.* (I went to one sandcutter what tell me say that my Aunt Hawa what witch me.) "I went to a sandcutter who told me that my Aunt Hawa put a curse on me." See also **moliman.**

**Sande:** [sãde] *n.,* A compulsory female initiation society found in many ethnic groups of Liberia, Guinea, and Sierra Leone. When girls reach adolescence they are isolated for a period of several weeks or months (formally years) in the Sande bush. As well as spiritual matters relating to ancestor veneration, during this period zoes (priests) teach them practical matters such as how to keep house, grow crops, and respect their future husbands. Before graduating the initiates must also undergo ritual scarification and cliterodectomy (female genital mutilation, also known by its initials FGM.) The Sande may also be called *women bush.* See also **poro, devil bush.**

**sangba:** [sãg͡ba] *n.,* A small drum played with the hands. Similar to a djembe. *Yu muh plea bring de sangba yeh so A can beat ih small.* (You must please bring the sangba here so I can beat it small.) "Please bring the drum here so I can play it for a little while."

**sasa:** [sasa] *n.,* A percussion instrument with a loud, sharp sound. Made from a gourd covered in a net of beads. Usually played by women. *Da woman can beat de sasa fine!* (That woman can beat the sasa fine!) "That woman plays the sasa well."

**sasabiya:** [sasabija] *n.,* Muslim prayer beads. From the Arabic *tasbil,* via the Mandingo language.

**sassy:** [sæsi] *adj.,* Rude, insolent, disrespectful, etc. *Da sassy geh ain geh tam fo school bisneh.* (That sassy girl ain't get time for school business.) "That insolent girl couldn't care less about school." See also **frisky.**

**sassywood:** [sasiwu] *n.,* 1. The poisonous bark of the Sassywood tree (*Erythrophlaeum guineensis*). In rural areas it is commonly made into a potion and used in traditional "trial by ordeal" hearings. The accused swears on the sassywood before ingesting it. Guilt or innocence is determined by their reaction to the poison. *De sassywood trow de man down skrate!* (The sassywood throw the man down straight!) "The sasswood knocked him out instantly!" 2. This term has also taken a broader meaning to include other trial by ordeals. For example, in some cases a machete, hot from being heated in a fire, is placed on the accused person's leg. If the accused flinches, he is presumed guilty. See also **kafu.**

**sassywood playa:** [sasiwu pleja] "sassywood player" *n.,* A diviner who determines truth by administering sassywood and interpreting the reaction of the accused.

**satisfy:** [satɪfaɪ] *v.,* To please, make happy. *De way da man do me, A ain satisfy.* (The way that man do me, I ain't satisfied.) "I am not happy with what that man did to me." This word is often said in the context of one's heart. *Ma heart satisfy na.* "My heart is satisfied now."

**sauches:** [sautʃes] "sausage" *n.,* Hot dog. A popular street food in Monrovia. *Ih doh nyoung boys dem wa can be selling sauches on de ro.* (It those young boys them what can be selling sausages on the road.) "It's those young boys who sell hot dogs on the street."

**sawasaw:** [sawəsaw] "soursop" *n.,* Soursop. *Annona muricata.* The tree has a green, spiky, football-sized fruit with a white creamy pulp. *Doh reh ans* *all on my soursaw tree.* (Those red ants all on my soursaw tree.) "My soursop tree is covered in those red ants."

**sawasawa:** [sawasawa] "sour-sour" *n.*, Jamaican red sorrel. *Hibiscus sabdariffa.* The okra-like pod of this plant is enjoyed in sauces for its pungent taste. The dried flowers are also used to make a sweet, cold drink. *Wen de sawasawa fut, A coming mek ih wif* soup. (When the sour-sour full, I coming make it with soup.) "When the sour sour are ripe, I will make a soup with them."

**say:** [se] 1. *v.*, Used to preface a quote. *Awa moda tell uh say, 'Yor muh na ditey yo clo'.* (Our mother tell us say, 'Y'all must not dirty your clothes.') "Our mother told us, 'You all should not get your clothes dirty.'" 2. *pro.*, Can also be used as a relative pronoun to introduce a clause, as with the Standard English "that." *De mechanic tell me say my battery fini.* (The mechanic tell me say my battery finish.) "The mechanic told me that my battery is dead."

**scary:** [skɛɹi] *adj.*, To be afraid. *Wen a yeh de rogue to de door, A wa too scary.* (When I hear the rogue to the door, I was too scary.) "I was very scared when I heard the robber at the door."

**scent:** [sɛ̃] *n.*, Used rather than odor, smell, etc. *He tell me say he ain lek bushmeat rotting scent.* (He tell me say he ain't like bushmeat rotting scent.) "He told me he doesn't like bushmeat's rotten smell."

**schnap:** [ʃnæp] *n.*, A unit of measurement for liquid equaling approximately eight ounces. The term comes from "Schnapps" –a brand of alcohol available throughout Liberia in small eight ounce bottles. *Ma, yu muh plea gii me two schnap kerosene.* (Ma, you must please give me two schnap kerosene.) "Mother, please give me eight ounces of kerosene."

**school fee:** [sku fi] *n.*, Used rather than "tuition." *De paren dem cyan pay deh chiren school fee. Da wa mek ih de teacha weak to go to school.* (The parent them cannot pay the children school fee. That what make it the teachers weak to go to school.) "The parents don't pay their kids tuition. That's why the teachers are unmotivated to work at the school."

**scrash back:** [skɹæʃ bæk˺] "scratch back" *v.*, To give a bribe. See **co wata, knock belly.**

**scrash farm:** [skɹæʃ fa:m] "scratch farm" *v.*, To hoe in preparation for planting or weeding. Generally considered women's work. *Lorpu go scrash farm today. Tomorrow she will go broadcast de seed.* (Lorpu go scratch farm today. Tomorrow she will go broadcast the seed.) "Lorpu went to hoe the farm today. Tomorrow she will sow the seeds."

**sea:** [si] *n.*, Used rather than "ocean." *Doh Fanti fishermen dem can be owa de sea hoday een deh big big keenu.* (Those Fanti fisherman them can be on the sea whole day in their big big canoe.) "Those Fanti fishermen are always on the ocean in their big canoes."

**sea chicken:** [si t͡ʃikĩ] Trigger Fish. *Balistes spp.* A type of ocean fish, valued for food in Liberia.

**sea bat:** [si bæt'] *n.,* The Manta Ray. *Manta spp.*

**sea cow:** [si kau] *n.,* See **water cow.**

**sea monkey:** [si mɔ̃kɛ] *n.,* A whale. Many stories can be heard in Liberia about "sea monkeys" that wash up on the beach. People collect large quantities of meat from the carcass before the tide carries the whale back to sea the next day.

**sea side:** [si saɪ] *n.,* A reference to the coastal areas of Liberia which is generally more developed than the interior. *De goo goo school dem plenty to de sea side den de interior.* (The good good school them plenty to the sea side than the interior.) "There are a lot more good schools in the coastal towns than in the interior."

**secret:** [sikɹɛ] *n.,* Powerful knowledge hidden from the general public. Often used in reference to occultic knowledge and sacred oaths.

**secret society:** [sikɹɛ sosaɪti] *n.,* A general reference to the power associations found in all strata of Liberian society. Examples include the **Poro** and **Sande** for rural Liberians and the Freemasons for the Americo-Liberian ruling class. All secret societies involve initiation rites, expected codes of conduct and secret signs. See **sign.**

**see:** [si] *v.,* To get, to receive. *A ain see!* (I ain't see!) "I did not receive any!"

**seed:** [si] *n.,* 1. Game pieces for a board game. *De tam A win de man, he geh vex an wase de seed all on de groun.* (The time I win the man, he get vex and waste the seed all on the ground.) "When I beat the man, he got mad and threw the game pieces all over the floor." 2. Testicles. *Da man sheep seed too long long.* (The man sheep seed too long long.) "That ram's testicles are very long." 3. Due to the influence of what many in the West refer to the "Prosperity Gospel," this word is also used metaphorically in charismatic churches to refer to money given in expectation of the greater "harvest" that it will produce. *A fini sow my hundreh dala seed to de church. A jus waiting to see ha Goh going bless me.* (I finish sow my hundred dollar seed to the church. I just waiting to see how God going bless me.) "I have given my hundred dollar at the church. I'm just waiting to see how God is going to bless me."

**sef (1):** [sɛf] "self" *pro.,* 1. For one's self. Added to personal pronouns for emphasis, *Ih my own sef chicken wa we coming cook fo de feas.* (It my own self chicken what we coming cook for the feast.) "It's my very own chickens that we will cook for the feast." This word can be redoubled for emphasis to mean "one's very own self." *Da my sef sef wa been suffring fron running stomach.* (That my self self what been suffering from running stomach.) "It's me myself who has been having problems with diarrhea."

**sef** (2): [sɛf] "self" *adv.,* Similar usage to the Standard English "even." Inserted on the end of a negative clause for emphasis. *Da woman na know cooking bisneh. She cyan fis pototo green sef!* (That woman not know cooking business. She can't fix potato green self!) 'That woman doesn't know how to cook. She can't even make potato greens!"

**sen:** [sɛ̃] "send" *v.,* To pass the ball in a game. *Junior sen de ball to Eddie. Den Eddie score goal.* (Junior send the ball to Eddie. Then Eddie score goal.) "Junior passed the ball to Eddie. Then Eddie scored a goal."

**sense:** [sɛ̃s] *n.,* Intelligence, cleverness, wits. *De way da pekin toking soon show he geh plenty sense.* (The way that pekin talking soon show he got plenty sense.) "The way that little boy is talking so early shows that he is very intelligent." See also **cleva.**

**serious:** [siɹus] *adj.,* Level-headed, sincere, committed. *Doh chiren ain serious fo school bisneh. Hoday dey jus passing all roun.* (Those children ain't serious for school business. Whole day they just passing all round.) "Those kids aren't interested in their schooling. They are always just roaming around."

**set:** [sɛt'] *v.,* To wait in ambush. *De hunta wa setting for de lepor.* (The hunter was setting for the leopard.) "The hunter was waiting in ambush for the leopard."

**sexing:** [sɛksĩ] *v.,* Sleeping around, engaging in illicit sex. Also known as **loving.** *Junior can always be sexing to different different gehs.* (Junior can always be sexing to different different girls.) "Junior is always sleeping around with a lot of different girls."

**shades:** [ʃeds] *n.,* Used rather than "sunglasses." *John can jus be wearing doh fine fine shades to be bluffing.* (John can just be wearing those fine fine shades to be bluffing.) "John wears those nice sunglasses just to impress people."

**shako:** [ʃako] *v.,* To dress in fashionable clothes. Slang. *A will shako befo A go to da geh hus.* (I will shako before A go to that girl house.) "I will dress up before I go to that girl's house." See also **zoot** and **blade.**

**shadow:** [ʃædo] *n.,* In addition to the Standard English usage, this word can also refer to a reflection in a mirror or water.

**shame**: [ʃem] *adj.*, Ashamed, embarrassed. *Peter shame to come een town since dey see heen wif da geh.* (Peter shame to come in town since they see him with that girl.) "Peter is ashamed to come to town since they saw him together with that girl."

**sharp**: [ʃap] "sharp" *v.*, To sharpen. *De file leave to de hus, so A fine rock to sharp de cutlass.* (The file leave to the house, so I find rock to sharp the cutlass.) "The file was left at the house, so I found a rock to sharpen the cutlass on."

**sheengun**: [ʃingᴧ̃] "chewing gum" *n.*, Little children can often be heard asking, *Yu muh gii me sheengun, yah?* (You must give me chewing gum, you hear?) "You will give me chewing gum, OK?"

**sheet**: [ʃitˀ] *n.*, Used only in reference to a sheet of paper. The cloth used to cover a bed is called *bed sheet.*

**shine-shine**: [ʃãʃã] *adj.*, Used to describe clothes adorned with reflective fabric or beading. *Ain yu see Patience shako to de club een huh shine-shine clo?* (Ain't you see Patience shako to the club in her shine-shine clothes?) "Didn't you see Patience all dressed up at the club in her shiny clothes?"

**shop**: [ʃap] *n.*, A small dry-goods business, found in urban neighborhoods as well as villages. Usually owned by local merchants. They stock such items such as candles, matches, crackers and canned goods. Distinguished from the larger **store**.

**show**: [ʃo] *v.*, To justify one's self, to prove that one is superior. *De way Decontee wan spoil my name, A will show mysef to hur!* (The way Decontee want spoil my name, I will show myself to her!) "Decontee wants to ruin my reputation, but I will show that I am better than her."

**shu be**: [ʃu bi] "should be" *adv.*, Used rather than "probably is." *Korpu shu be roun elewen yeah ole.* (Korpu should be around eleven year old.) "Korpu is probably around eleven years old."

**shulla**: [ʃᴧɾᴧ] "shut up" *v.*, Be quite, keep it down. Not considered rude. *Yor shulla na!* (Y'all shut up now!) "Everybody, be quiet!"

**sick bush**: [sɪk buɪʃ] *n.*, A secret enclosure in the forest used by zoes to conduct healing rituals. *De tam he wa to de sick bush, he see de zoe change wif snek.* (The time he was to the sick bush, he see the zoe change with snake.) "When he was in the sick bush, he saw the witch doctor transform into a snake."

**side**: [saɪ] 1. *n.*, Area, place. *Wa side yu stopping dee few day?* (What side you stopping these few day?) "Where are you living these days?"

144

2. *prep.*, Beside, near. *A meh Flomo stanning side de ro.* (I met Flomo standing side the road.) "I found Flomo standing near the road."

**siddon:** [sɪdãũ] "sit down" *v.,* To sit. *A saw de woman siddon side de ro crying.* (I saw the women sit down side the road crying.) "I saw the woman sitting by the side of the road crying."

**sign** (1): [sãj] *n.,* A signal used to communicate between members of the same secret society. *Dey wa coming chunk de man een jail, buh he trow sign to de judge so dey free heen.* (They was coming chunk the man in jail, but he throw sign to the judge so they free him.) "The judge was going to throw the man in jail, but he gave a secret signal to the judge so he was let go."

**sign** (2): [sãj] *n.,* A seedling. *She coming take de coconuh sign an plant ih een her yar.* (She coming take the coconut sign and plant it in her yard.) "She's going to plant the coconut seedling in her yard."

**signboard:** [sãjbo] *n.,* Used rather than sign, billboard, road sign, etc. *Dey puh one nyew signboard side de ro to de junshun.* (They put one new signboard side the road to de junction.) "They put up a new sign by the road at the intersection."

**sinner:** [sɪnɔ] *adj.,* In addition to its Christian usage, this word may be heard in rural areas in reference to a person who refuses initiation into the secret societies.

**sirees:** [sɪɹis] *n.,* A colloqual term for American English—a dialect considered nearly unintelligible to many rural Liberians. *De man can be speaking so so sireese. He cyan speak de clear English.* (The man can be speaking so so sireese. He can't speak the clear English.) "The man only speaks the American dialect. He doesn't speak clear English."

**sista:** [sista] "sister" *n.,* 1. Used to refer to any female relative of the speaker's generation. 2. A term of respect used when addressing women of the speaker's generation.

**sitting down:** [sɪfi dã] *v.,* To rest, to be inactive. *De docta say A muh be sitting down till de malaria can fini.* (The doctor say I must be sitting down till the malaria can finish.) "The doctor said I must rest until the malaria is over."

**sitting fee:** [sɪfi fi] *n.,* Money paid to participants of an workshop or conference for attending the event.

**skrate:** [skɹet˺] "straight" adv., Straightaway, immediately. *Wen A yeh de lepor coming, A wake up skrate.* (When I hear the leopard coming, I wake up straight.) "When I heard the leopard coming, I got up immediately."

**skubee**: [skubi] *n.*, Sneakers. Tennis shoes.

**sleep**: [slip] *v.*, To stay overnight. Often said of inanimate objects. *Yo car coming sleep yeh tonight?* (Your car coming sleep here tonight?) "Are you leaving your car here for the night?"

**sleeping suit**: [slipī su] *n.*, Pajamas.

**slippa**: [slɪpɔ] "slipper" *n.*, Flip-flops, thongs. *De tam A wa walking een de bush my slippa cut.* (The time I was walking in the bush my slipper cut.) "When I was walking in the forest my flip-flops broke."

**slippery soup**: [slɪpɹɛ sup] *n.*, A sauce made from dried meat and bitter balls. Served with **GB**.

**small**: [smau] *adv.*, A little. *A coming lay don small.* (I coming lay down small.) "I'm going to lie down for a little while."

**small boy**: [smau bɔɪ] *n.*, A servant, a person of little consequence or social standing, a nobody. *A na yo small boy so A muh be doing yo wok fo yu.* (I not your small boy so I must be doing your work for you.) "I am not your servant that I should be doing your work for you."

**small boy unit**: [smau bɔɪ junɪ] *n.*, Groups of child soldiers who fought during Liberia's civil war. Children as young as six years old were drugged and forced to commit atrocities to prove loyalty to their commanders.

**small mo**: [smau mo] "small more" *adj.*, Almost. *A wa too sick! Small mo A wa coming die.* (I was too sick! Small more I was coming die.) "I was very sick! I almost died." See also **leave small**.

**small small**: [smau smau] *adv.*, 1. Little by little, gradually. *He getting betta small small.* (He getting better small small.) "He's gradually getting better." 2. Slowly. *Jus be going small small so you cyan distup de alligato.* (Just be going small small so you can't disturb the alligator.) "Just go slowly so you don't upset the crocodile."

**small small ting**: [smau smau tĩ] *idiom.*, A euphemism that can be used in a wide range of situations when the subject matter is uncomfortable. *De teacha say A muh be doing small small ting wif heen befo A can pass to de nes grade.* (The teacher say I must be doing small small thing with him before I can pass to the next grade.) "The teacher said I have to sleep with him if I want to pass to the next grade."

**snapper**: [snapɔ] *n.*, Refers to a large, ocean-going canoe. Often painted colorfully and adorned with religious slogans. Powered by an outboard motor.

**sneaker**: [snikɔ] *n.*, Used rather than "tennis shoes." Also called **skubee**.

**snek fish:** [snek fiʃ] "snake fish" *n.*, 1. The bichir. *Polypterus spp.* A eel-like fish with a hard, scaly exterior and sharp dorsal spines. Notable for its ability to breath air. If the ground is sufficiently moist this fish is able to crawl on land from one water source to another. 2. This term can also refer to a variety of fresh and saltwater eel species.

**so:** [so] *adv.*, 1. The directional "there." *De ole ma go so.* (The old ma go so.) "The old woman went over there." 2. As it is. *Leh ih stay so.* (Let it stay so.) "Let it stay as it is." 3. In that way, like that, about. *Wa yu toking so?* (What you talking so?) "What are you talking about?"

**soak:** [sokˈ] *v.*, To pummel, beat. *Ifan yu ain move fron yeh, A coming soak yu!* (If you ain't move from here, I coming soak you!) "If you don't get out of here, I'm going to beat you!"

**soak tongue:** [sokˈ toŋ] *v.*, To drink to the point of intoxication. Slang. *Salimu go to de cane juice shop to soak hih tongue.* (Salimu go to the cane juice shop to soak his tongue.) "Salimu went to the cane liquor stand to get drunk."

**society:** [sosaɪti] *n.*, Most often heard in reference to a secret society.

**society bush:** [sosaɪti buɪʃ] *n.*, See **devil bush, Poro** and **Sande.**

**society man:** [sosaɪti mẽ] *n.*, See **heartman.**

**softly-softly** (1): [sɔflisɔfli] *n.*, The potto. *Perodictius potto.* A slow-moving, nocturnal primate akin to the loris. It is believed locally that they can choke monkeys to death with their hands, giving rise to the common proverb, "Softly-softly catch a monkey." Considered by many to be a taboo food for pregnant women. *Woman wa geh belly muh na eat softly-softly befo she born ugly baby.* (Woman what got belly must not eat softly-softly before she born ugly baby.) "A pregnant woman should not eat potto meat or her baby will be ugly."

**softly-softly** (2): [sɔflisɔfli] *adv.*, Slowly, gently, carefully. *Jus be woking softly-softly so you cyan wake uh de baby.* (Just be walking softly-softly so you can't wake up the baby.) "Just walk very gently so you don't wake the baby."

**solong:** [solõ] "so long" *adv.*, So long as, as long as. Used in forming conditional clauses. *Solong my ma stih yeh, A ain going cook.* (So long my ma is here, I ain't going cook.) "As long as my mother is here, I will not cook."

**some:** [sÃ] *adv.*, *pro.*, Used rather than the Standard English "any." *A ain geh some.* (I ain't got some.) "I don't have any."

**some kina way**: [sʌ̃ kina we] "some kind of way" *adj.*, Unpleasant, undesirable. *Da woman too some kina way.* (That woman too some kind of way.) "That woman is very unpleasant."

**sometamly**: [sʌ̃taɪmli] "sometimely" *adj.*, Used rather than moody, temperamental, etc. *Da geh too sometamly. Today de ting A say mek hur laugh, tomorrow ih will mek hur cry.* (That girl too sometimely. Today the thing I say make her laugh, tomorrow it will make her cry.) "That girl is very moody. The things I say to her make her laugh today, but tomorrow the same things will make her cry."

**someting**: [sʌ̃ti] "something" *n.*, 1. Used rather than "thing" in reference to an unspecified object. *A coming go geh my someting to de hus.* (I coming go get my something to the house.) "I am going to go get my thing at the house." 2. Often used when the name of the given object has been forgotten, similar to the American English nonsense word "thingamajig." *Ih da someting deh.* (It the something there.) "It's that thingamajig over there" 3. This word may also be used when it is dangerous to name the specific entity in question, such as a powerful forest spirit. *Malawolo shu geh someting behin heen wa can mek ih he kill plenty meat.* (Malawolo should get something behind him what can make it he kill plenty meat.) "Since Malawolo kills so many animals, he must have a spirit helping him hunt."

**soon**: [sū] *adj.*, Used rather than "early." *A luf to fishing soon een de moning. Da de tam de cyatfish dem can be too frisky.* (I love to fishing soon in the morning. That the time catfish them can be too frisky.) "I like to fish early in the morning. That's when the catfish are very active."

**sore**: [so] *n.*, A general reference to any cut or open wound. *De docta gii me plasta to cowa my sore.* (The doctor give me plastic to cover my sore.) "The doctor gave me a bandage to cover my wound."

**sorrowful**: [saɹafɔ] *adj.*, Sad, pitiful. *De ole ma crying sorrowful way.* (The old ma crying sorrowful way.) "The old lady is crying in a very pitiful way."

**sorry**: [saɹi] *adj.*, Different usage than in Standard English. Whereas in Standard English this word can be used to express empathy or sympathy for someone, in Liberian English it generally implies guilt or responsibility. See also **newa mine yah**.

**so so**: [soso] *adj.*, Only, exclusively, without exception. *Deh so so bittaball to de garden.* (There so so bitterball to the garden.) "There are only bitterballs in the garden.

**S-O-SO**: [ɛs o so] *n.*, A common method of teaching basic phonetics to Liberian schoolchildren. The teacher gives the consonant and vowel separately, then together and the children repeat afterwards. For example, S-O-SO, T-O-To...

**soun**: [saũ] "sound" *adj.*, To be in ones right mind. *Fron de tam de war fini, da man na been soun.* (From the time the war finish, that man not been sound.) "Since the war finished, that man has not been in his right mind."

**soun horn**: [saũ hõ] "sound horn" *v.*, Used in reference to a vehicle's horn instead of honk, beep, etc. *De peepo wa pack up een de ro, so de driva soun hih horn.* (The people was pack up in the road, so the driver sound his horn.) "A group of people were on the road, so the driver blew his horn."

**soup**: [sup] *n.*, A sauce served over rice. Each tribe in Liberia is known for a particular sauce. The Vai like **cassava leaf**, the Lorma **torbagee**, the Gio **palm butta**, etc. *Hoday yu fising dis same soup. Yu na know different one?* (Whole day you fixing this same soup. You not know different one?) "You're always making the same kind of sauce. Don't you know how to make any other kind?"

**soup kind**: [sup kãj] *n.*, Ingredients for making sauce. *When A een town A will buy de soup kind.* (When I in town I will buy the soup kind.) "When I'm in town I will buy the ingredients for sauce." See **chicken soup**, **Manpo**, **greens** and **red oil**.

**soya boid**: [soja boɪ] "soldier bird" *n.*, Another name for the **rice bird**, referencing they way they "attack" rice fields like soldiers.

**soyaman**: [sojamɛ̃] "soldier man" *n.*, A common term for a government soldier. *One soyaman wa standing to de markeh wif hih gbala.* (One soldier man was standing to the market with his gbala) "A soldier was standing in the market with his weapon."

**speed**: [spid] *n.*, The phrase "get speed" means to be a flirt, good with the ladies, etc. *Daniel geh speed o!* (Daniel get speed o!) "Daniel is a big flirt."

**spell**: [spɛ] *n.*, Epilepsy. *Da boy suffring fron spell. He can drop any tam.* (That boy suffering from spell. He can drop any time.) "That boy has problems with epilepsy. He can fall down at any time."

**Spida story**: [spaɪdɔ stoɹi] "Spider story" *n.*, Many traditional Liberian stories feature Spider, a wily character who uses trickery to manipulate the other animals in the stories. Used to teach morals and cultural values. *A wan tell yor one Spida story about ha Spida geh hih tin waist.* (I want to tell y'all one Spider story about how Spider get his thin waist.) "I want to tell you all a Spider story about why Spider has a thin waist."

**spirit**: [spiɹɪ] *n.*, May refer to a number of supernatural beings such as ancestor spirits, forest spirits and **jina**.

**spitting snek**: [spɪfi snek˺] "spitting snake" *n.*, The spitting cobra. Some species (i.e. *Naga goldii*) are actually capable of spitting venom into the eyes of their prey or enemies to blind them.

**spoil**: [spoɪ] *v.*, 1. Used rather than ruin, break, damage, etc. *Tek tam befo you spoil de tarpoline.* (Take time before you spoil the tarpaulin.) "Watch out or you will ruin the tarp." *De car spoil ewasince.* (The car spoil ever since.) "The car has been broken for a long time." 2. Can be used colloquially in a positive sense. *Da man really spoil de drum.* (The man really spoil the drum.) "That man can play the drum well!"

**spoil mouf**: [spoɪ mauf] *idiom.*, To eat heavily and with gusto. *Wen my boifday come we all coming spoil awa mouf!* (When my birthday come we all going to spoil our mouth!) "When my birthday comes around we are going to pig out!"

**spring frog**: [spɹ̃i fɹɔ] *n.*, This term refers to several varieties of edible frog smaller than a bullfrog.

**spy**: [spaɪ] *v.*, 1. To see, observe. *A spy de woman running coming.* (I spy the woman running coming.) "I saw the woman running to come here." See also **witness**. 2. To sneak a peak. Often heard in reference to cheating on a test. *De tam yor teking de test, yor muh na spy yo fren sheet yeh?* (The time you taking the test, you must not spy your friend sheet, you hear?) "When you are taking the test, you should not cheat by looking at your friend's paper."

**stay**: [ste] *adv.*, An auxiliary used to indicate the continuation of a situation. May be pronounced "stedi" by some speakers. *De car stay to de garage.* (The car stay to the garage.) "The car is still at the mechanic's shop." Also: *De rain stay coming till de riwa fut.* (The rain stay coming till the river full.) "The rain kept on coming till the river was flooded."

**staylong**: [stelɔ̃] "stay long" *v.*, 1. To spend a long period of time doing something or being at a place. *He ain staylohn to de clinic.* (He ain't stay long to the clinic.) "He didn't stay a long time at the clinic. 2. To last, endure. *Mudstick hus cyan staylohn.* (Mudstick house can't stay long.) "Mudstick houses don't last long."

**stick**: [stɪk˺] *n.*, A piece of unsawn wood. Can reference anything from a twig to log. *De stick dey puh across dis creek spoil ewasince.* (The stick they put across this creek spoil ever since.) "The log they put across this creek (for a bridge) rotted a long time ago." For cut wood, see **plank**.

**sticky plaster**: [stɪk˺i plastɔ] *n.*, 1. A Band-Aid or other adhesive medical tape. *A wan go to de clinih so dey can gii me sticky plasto fo dis sore.* (I want go to the clinic so they can give me sticky plaster for this sore.) "I want to go to the clinic so they can give me a band-aid for this sore." 2.

A person who hangs around uselessly. *We all wa on de projec, buh Tarnu pa wa one sticky plaster.* (We all were on the project, but Tarnu part was one sticky plaster.) "All of us were working on the project, but Tarnu was hanging around uselessly."

**stinger:** [stĩɔ] *n.,* Stingray. *Dasyatis spp.* Valued for food in Liberia.

**stink-mouf:** [stĩ mɔf] "stink-mouth" *n.,* Foul language, abusive talk. *Da man stay putting hih stink-mouf on me, so A blow heen een de stomac.* (The man stay putting his stink-mouth on me, so I blow him in the stomach.) "That man kept insulting me, so I punched him in the stomach."

**store:** [sto] *n.,* A relatively large general goods establishment, often run by foreigners such as Lebanese, Indians or Fulanis. Distinguished from the small neighborhood **shop**.

**stranga:** [stɹẽʒa] "stranger" *n.,* A guest, visitor. *We geh stranger to de house dee few days.* (We got stranger to the house these few days.) "We have had a guest staying at our house recently."

**stranga fada/moda:** [stɹẽʒa fada] "stanger father/mother" *n.,* A godparent, a host/hostess. A non-relative who looks out for the well-being of a newcomer without family connections in the area. *Ma stranga moda buy one fine lappa suit fo me dis yeah."* (My stranger mother buy one fine lappa suit for me this year.) "My godmother bought a nice African suit for me this year."

**stranga son/daughta:** [stɹẽʒa sã] "stranger son/daughter" *n.,* The person being cared for by the "stranger" father or mother.

**stupid:** [stupɪ] *adj.,* 1. Lacking sense, foolish. A strong insult. *Yu say A stupid? Why yu wan cauz me so?* (You say I'm stupid? Why you want curse me so?) "You calling me stupid? Why would you insult me like that?" 2. To be complacent, not interested in exploiting a situation. *Da Kpelle man geh da goo goo position, buh he ain do notting goo fo heensef. Fo true Kpelle man stupid.* (That Kpelle man get the good good position, but he ain't do nothing good for himself. For true Kpelle man stupid.) "That Kpelle man got that great position, but he didn't he take advantage of it (i.e. behave in a corrupt manner.) It's true. Kpelle people are complacent."

**suck teet:** [sʌk titˀ] "suck teeth" *v.,* A sign of contempt. *Sammy suck hih teet at Peter de way he wa acting stupid so.* (Sammy such his teeth at Peter the way he was acting stupid so.) "Sammy sucked his teeth at Peter because he was acting stupid."

**suffa:** [sʌfa] "suffer" *v.,* To cause hardship or difficulty. Can refer to a truly terrible ordeal, as well as minor inconveniences. Unlike Standard English, this verb is often transitive in Liberian English (taking a subject.) *De* *man rally suffa me o!* (The man really suffer me o!) "The man really made me suffer!"

**suppose**: [sopos] *v.,* Used rather than 'what if' and 'supposing.' *Suppose A come nes week. Yu will still be deh?* (Suppose I come next week. You will still be there?) "What if I come next week. Will you still be there?"

**suppose to**: [sopos to] *adv.,* A hortative marker used rather than "ought to." *Willie suppose to be feeding de chicken, buh he go to play wif hih fren dem.* (Willie suppose to be feeding the chickens, but he go to play with his friends them.) "Willie ought to be feeding the chickens, but instead he went to play with his friends."

**sure case**: [ʃo kes] *adj.,* Used rather than surely, for sure, rest assured, etc. *Sure case ba ting will happen if we don stop da man.* (Sure case bad thing will happen if we don't stop that man.) "Rest assured bad things will happen if we don't stop that man."

**susu**: [susu] *n.,* A money cooperative. An informal system of banking for petty business owners. From the Yuruba language. Also called a **kuu**.

**swallow**: [swalo] *v.,* 1. Used to refer to the eating of certain foods, especially those made from cassava dough. **Dumboy** and **GB** are meant to be formed into balls and swallowed, rather than chewed. *Precious come to my hus to swallow fufu.* "Precious came to my house to swallow fufu." 2. To spiritually consume the soul of another through occultic power. *De tam A wa een de Poro bush, de devil swallow me.* (The time I was in the Poro bush, the devil swallow me.) "When I was being initiated in the Poro bush, the great forest spirit consumed my spirit."

**swamp lily**: [swam lɪli] *n.,* Various species of lilies in the *Crinum* genus which grow in Liberia's rivers and wetlands and bloom with a beautiful white blossom.

**swamp monkey**: [swam mɔ̃kɛ] *n.,* The Olive colobus. *Procolobus verus.* An olive colored monkey with a white underbelly and black face.

**swamp rice**: [swam raɪs] *n.,* The variety of rice grown in swamps and patties. The other common variety is **upland rice**.

**swear**: [swɛ] 1. *v.,* To make an oath or vow. *De goat swear de monkey he won enta de fores again.* (The goat swear the monkey he won't enter the forest again.) "The goat vowed to the monkey that he would never go into the forest again." 2. *Interj.,* The phrase "I swear" is used similarly to the American English, "I'll be damned" "You don't say," etc.

**swearin suit**: [sweɪ su] "swearing-in suit" *n.,* A short-sleaved, tailored suit and pants set. Traditionally worn at government "swearing-in ceremonies." *George look too fine today in hih swearin suit.* (George look too fine today in his swearing-in suit.) "George looks very nice today in his swearing-in suit."

**sweet:** [swi] *adj.,* Very tasty, delicious. Does not imply a sugary taste. *Dis fufu too sweet o!* (This fufu too sweet!) "This fufu is delicious!"

**sweet een yo mouf:** [swi ĩ jo mɔf] "sweet in your mouth" *idiom.,* Something that is pleasing or enjoyable, and thus often repeated. *Dis yo woman bisneh sweet een yo mouf na, buh soon ih will gii yu haad tam.* (This your woman business sweet in your mouth now, but soon it will give you hard time.) "Your womanizing is enjoyable at the moment, but later you will reap the consequences."

**sweet-mouf:** [swi mɔf] "sweet mouth" *n.,* Flattery, sweet talk. *A wa na coming do ih, buh den she puh her sweet-mouf on me.* (I was not coming do it, but then she put her sweet mouth on me.) "I wasn't going to do it, but then she flattered me."

**swell:** [swɛ] *n.,* Waves in the oceans, surf. *De tam A wa stanning side de sea, de swell come up an soak my trousa.* (The time I was standing side the sea, the swell come up and soak my trousers.) "When I was standing on the beach, the wave came up and soaked my pants."

**swella:** [swɛla] "swelled up" *adj.,* Swollen. *Torn juke hih foot. Ih na swella ba way.* (Thorn juke his foot. It now swell up bad way.) "A thorn pierced his foot. Now it has become very swollen."

# T

**tableh:** [tablɛ] "tablet" *n.*, Used rather than "pill." *A coming go to de docta to geh pain tableh.* (I coming go to the doctor to get pain tablet.) "I'm going to the doctor to get pain pills."

**taboo:** [tæbu] *n.*, See **law**.

**tactic:** [tætɪkˀ] *n,.*, A trick or strategy to accomplish a given end. *A scary to aks ma pa to credih me money, buh Alfred know de correc tactic.* (I scary to ask my dad to credit me money, but Alfred know the correct tactic.) "I am afraid to ask my dad to lend me money, but Alfred knows the right strategy."

**tactic pekin:** [tætɪkˀ pikī] *n.*, A person who knows the correct strategy to accomplish a given end.

**talah:** [tala] *n.*, A unit for measuring alcohol. Approximately one pint.

**tam:** [tã] "time" *n.*, 1. A turn in a game. *Da yo tam na.* (That your time now.) "It's your turn now." 2. Sexual climax, orgasm.

**tam lek dis:** [tam laɪ dɪ] "time like this" *adj.*, Refers to a similar time of day as the one in reference. *Tam lek dis A go to de wataside, buh A ain kill fish.* (Time like this I go to the waterside, but I ain't kill fish.) "I went to the river at this same time of day, but I didn't catch any fish."

**tam wa:** [tam wa] "time what" *adv.*, Often used rather than "when." *Da ting happing de tam when we wa to Guinea.* (The thing happen the time when we was to Guinea.) "That thing happened when we were in Guinea."

**Tank Goh:** [ten gɔ] "Thank God" *interj.*, Liberians tend to be very religious people and often use this phrase in response to inquiries about one's wellbeing.

**tank yu:** [ten ju] "thank you" *interj.*, Used in a broader sense than in Standard English to mean things such as "Good job!" "I'm happy for you!" "Congratulations!" etc. *Yo lappa suit fine. Tank yu!* (Your lappa suit fine. Thank you!) "Your lappa suit is nice. Good job picking it out."

**tape:** [tep] *n.*, A cassette player. The tape it plays is called a **cassette**. *My fren tape spoil, so we cyan lisen to music agin.* (My friend tape spoil, so we can't listen to music again.) "My friend's cassette player is broken, so we can't listen to music anymore."

**tar:** [ta:] *n.*, Heroin. *Da pure tar de rebo dem wa smoking.* (That pure tar the rebel them was smoking.) "That's pure heroin the rebels were smoking."

**tata:** [tata] *n.*, The vagina. The female sexual organ. See also **toto**.

**tausenleg**: [tauzɛnlɛg] "thousand-leg" *n.*, A millipede. Often refers to the African Giant Black Millipede, *Archispirostreptus gigas,* which can grow up to eleven inches in length. These millipedes secrete a defensive toxin that can cause a severe allergic reaction.

**taxi**: [tɛsi] *n.*, Used rather than "cab" and refers to any car used to transport paying passengers. Most taxis in Monrovia are painted yellow, but some are unmarked.

**tear-tear**: [tɛtɛ] *adj.*, Tattered. Often heard in reference to clothes or bills. Because the current currency system of Liberia has no coins, lower denomination get worn out quickly. Excessively tattered or torn Liberian dollars are rejected in the market. These are bought by collectors at a reduced rate, then redeemed at a bank. *A cyan hold dis tear-tear money. Yu muh plea bring noda one.* (I cannot hold this tear-tear money. You must please bring another one.) "I can't take this tattered bill. Please give me a different one."

**teet**: [tit˺] *n.*, Teeth. *Ma teet highting ba way!* (My teeth hurting bad way!) "My teeth are killing me!"

**telegraph line**: [tɛlɛgɹaf laĩ] *n.*, A hand-line used by fisherman on the open ocean.

**tendatenda**: [tẽdatẽda] "tender tender" *adj.*, Irresponsible, careless. *Yu tengatenga geh, yu betta tek tam.* (You tender tender girl, you better take time.) "You irresponsible girl, you better be careful."

**tek baf**: [te bæf] "take bath" *v.*, 1. To bathe. Liberians often bathe twice a day with scalding hot water. *Yu ain wan tek baf na?* (You ain't want take bath now?) "Don't you want to bathe now?" 2. To swim. *Me an my fren dem going tek baf to de sea.* (Me and my friend them going take bath to the sea.) "My friends and I are going to swim in the ocean.

**tek tam**: [te tam] "take time" *v.*, Be careful, watch out. *Tek tam befo yo spoil de catoon.* (Take time before you spoil the cartoon.) "Be careful that you don't ruin the box."

**tenik**: [tenik˺] "technique" *n.*, Manipulation, a scam. Often refers to making money through an illicit means. *All de plenty NGO you see yeh, da so so tenik.* (All the plenty NGO you see here, that so so tenik.) "All the NGO's you see are here only exist to make money for their employees."

**terms**: [tɛms] *n.*, Big words. *Saar wan show he know book fo true de way he toking do terms dem.* (Saar want show he know book for true the way he talking those terms them.) "Saar wants to show he is educated by the way he is talking with those big words."

156

**teteh:** [tete] *n.,* Breast. Rural Liberians traditionally hold to a different standard of modesty than Westerners. Breastfeeding in public is very common, and it is considered acceptable for an older woman to work shirtless on the farm or in her yard. *Da beby wan suck teteh.* (That baby want suck teteh.) "That baby wants to nurse."

**teteh wata:** [tete wata] "teteh water" *n.,* Breast milk. *De woman teteh water coming fini.* (The woman teteh water coming finish.) "The woman's breast milk is drying up."

**ticklish:** [tiklɪʃ] *v.,* To tickle. *He grap de lil geh an star to ticklish hur.* (He grab the little girl and start to ticklish her.) "He caught the little girl and started to tickle her."

**tide soap:** [taɪ sop] *n.,* Used to refer to any powered detergent. Commonly sold in small packages in the market.

**tie:** [taɪ] *v.,* To commit under an oath. *He tie to de society, so he won tok ih secreh.* (He tie to the society, so he won't talk it secret.) "He is bound to the society, so he won't reveal it's secrets." 2. To bind through sorcery. *De zoe come to de village to tie de witch.* (The zoe come to the village to tie the witch.) 'The zoe came to the village to bind the power of the fetish."

**tie face:** [taɪ fes] *v.,* To show anger or disapproval on one's face. *Wen Gartee yeh da boy cauz heen, he tie hih face.* (When Gartee hear the boy curse him, he tie his face.) "When Gartee heard that boy insulting him, he tied his face."

**tiga:** [taɪgɔ] "tiger" *n.,* The Serval Cat. *Felis serval togoensis.* A medium sized feline with a tawny coat in a pattern of black stripes and spots. Quite rare in Liberia, but occasionally killed by hunters in the deep forest. True tigers do not exist in Liberia.

**tight:** [taɪt'] *adj.,* Compact, petite. *Nyama da shor, tight woman deh.* (Nyama that short, tight woman there.) "Nyama is that petite woman over there."

**tin:** [tĩ] *n.,* A common unit of measurement, especially for seed rice. The "tin" is often a five gallon oil or kerosene can with the lid removed. *He pa, he plan two tin to hih farm dis yeah.* (He part, he plant two tin to his farm this year.) "As for him, he planted two tins on his farm this year."

**tinapaw:** [tinapɔ] *n.,* "Tin Apple" Originally a brand name, this has since become a generic term for mackerel canned in tomato sauce. Also called **fish cup.**

**ting:** [tĩ] *pron.,* Something. An unspecified amount. *A see ting lek fifty chicken deh.* (I see thing like fifty chicken there.) "I saw something like fifty chickens there."

**tiya**: [taja] "tired" *adj.,* To be satisfied. Often heard in reference to eating. *De fufu sweet, buh fo true A tiya na.* (The fufu sweet, but for true I tired now.) "The fufu is delicious, but I really am full now."

**to**: [tu] *prep.,* Indicates the location of the subject in question. Used rather than at, on, etc. *She to de hus.* (She to the house.) "She's at the house."

**today person**: [tude pɔsẽ] *n.,* Somebody who embraces modern values. Open minded and in touch with the latest trends. It is commonly heard in a negative form as a means of peer pressure. *Mary, wa happen yu don wan go to de club? Fo true yu na today person!* (Mary, what happen you don't want to go to the club? For true you not today person.) "Mary, why don't you want to go to the night club? You really are old-fashioned!"

**toh**: [tɔ] *n.,* A dough made from reconstituted cassava flakes. The dough is formed into balls and served with a watery soup. Eaten primarily by the Mandingo.

**toileh**: [toɪlɛ] "toilet" *v.,* To defecate. *A ain know wa happing de chiren can toileh behin de hus so.* (I ain't know what happen the children can toilet behind the house so.) "I don't know why the children defecate behind the house like that."

**tok**: [tɔk˙] *v.,* 1. To say, to discuss. *A fini tok ih.* (I finish talk it.) "I've said all I have to say." 2. To make noise. Many animals and even inanimate objects are said to "talk" in Liberian English. *Doh bullfrog dem wa toking de ho night.* (Those bullfrog them was talking the whole night.) "Those bullfrogs were making noise all through the night."

**tomato color**: [tometo colɔ] *adj.,* Describes the lighter, often reddish, shade of skin possessed by some Liberians. *Francine da fine tomato color woman.* (Francine that fine tomato color woman) "Francine is that beautiful woman with light-reddish skin."

**too**: [tu] *adj.,* 1. Used rather than *very.* It does not indicate an excessive amount or degree as in Standard English. *De soup too sweet!* "The soup is very delicious!" 2. Also. *Weh my own too?* (Where my own too?) "Where's the one for me?"

**toodo**: [tudu] *n.,* Used when the speaker cannot remember the name of an object. *Yu muh bring da toodo wa sitting deh.* (You must bring that toodo what sitting there.) "Bring that watchamacallit that's sitting over there."

**torborgee**: [tɔbʌgi] *n.,* Refers to a variety of sauces made from soda, kitili and rancid red oil and served over rice. Associated primarily with the Lorma ethnic group of Lofa County. Not recommended for a Western palate. *A eat some torbagee las nightwa rally run my stomach.* (I eat some torbagee last night what really run my stomach.) "I ate some torba-gee last night that gave me bad diarrhea." See also **country salt**.

**torbagee oil**: [tɔbʌgi ɔj] *n.,* Palm oil purposely allowed to go rancid, giv-ing it a distinctive taste and odor. Used in torborgee dishes. *Ma aunty to de creek fising torbagee oil.* (My aunty to the creek fixing torborgee oil.) "My aunt is by the creek making torborgee oil."

**torbasoyee**: [tɔbʌsoji] *n.,* A kind of oil-based sauce prepared by the Kpelle. Similar to **torborgee**, but with less soda.

**torn**: [tɔ̃] "thorn" *n.,* Fish bones. *Tek tam so de fish torn muh na juke yu.* (Take time so the fish thorn must not juke you.) "Be careful that you don't get poked by the fish bones."

**torn-torn**: [tɔ̃tɔ̃] *n.,* A lot of thorns, a thorny patch. *Deh too mush torn-torn to Zuba farm.* (There too much torn-torn to Zuba farm.) "There are lots of thorn patches at Zuba's farm."

**torshlight**: [tɔʃlaɪ] "torch light" *n.,* A flashlight. *Shine de torshlight dis way.* (Shine the torch this way.) "Shine the flashlight this way."

**tote**: [tot˺] *v.,* To carry a load. Liberians often carry heavy burdens on their heads. *A tote de gallon fron all de way Zuwedru.* (I tote the gallon from all the way Zuwedru.) "I carried the container all the way from Zuwe-dru."

**toto**: [toto] *n.,* The male genitalia, the penis. *Da lil boy trouseh drop. Na hih toto showing.* (The little boy trouser drop. Now his toto showing.) "That little boy lost his pants. Now his privates are showing." See also **tata**.

**town**: [tã] *n.,* A permanent human settlement that is larger than a village and has a central market area. Whereas in Standard English a town generally refers to a community of over several thousand people, in Liberia much smaller communities may be called "towns." See also **city**.

**town chief**: [tã t͡ʃif] *n.,* A locally elected head of a village who presides over a council of elders to settle local disputes and represents the interests of the community to the clan chief, paramount chief and district commis-sioner.

**town owna**: [tã ona] "town owner" *n.,* The highest ranking representative of the founding lineage of a community. This man must be consulted along with the town chief before any important decisions affecting the community are made.

**traditional marriage**: [tɹadɪʃəna meɹɛ3] *n.,* A marriage conducted accord-ing to tribal customs, as opposed to a church or "civilized" marriage. Recognized by the Liberian government as being legally binding. See also **dowry**.

**trash**: [tɹaʃ] "thrush" *n.,* A term used to describe a number of fungal related conditions common to babies. May refer to white patches in the mouth, or particles in a baby's stool.

**tree bear**: [tʃɹi bɛ:] *n.,* See **tree goat**.

**tree goat**: [tʃɹi gotʼ] *n.,* The Tree Hyrax. *Dendrohyrax arboreus.* An arboreal, nocturnal mammel. Medium sized with an appearance resembling a rabbit without long ears. Males produce an increasingly loud screaming territorial call that can be heard from miles away.

**tree raccoon**: [tʃɹi rakū] *n.,* Most commonly, the African Palm Civet. *Nandinia binotata.* A small nocturnal mammal with a cat-like appearance, it has a tawny brown coat with dark spots and a long tail. This word can also reference other arboreal viverrids such as the genet and lingsang. May also be called **raccoon** or **bush cat**.

**tribe**: [tɹaɪb] *n.,* 1. An ethnic group who share a common history and language. The Liberian government officially recognizes sixteen tribes in Liberia, although many of these, especially in the south-east, can be broken down into smaller segments which speak languages unintelligible to others sections of their "tribe." 2. The language spoken by a particular ethnic group. *De two man wa toking, buh A cyan yeh deh tribe.* (The two men was talking, but I can't hear their tribe.) "The two men were talking, but I didn't understand their tribe's language."

**tricky**: [tɹɪki] *adj.,* Used rather than crafty, sneaky, ingenious, etc. *De tricky spida carry all de foo.* (The tricky spider carry all the food.) "The crafty spider took all the food." See also **katakata** and **Spida Story**.

**tricky jack**: [tɹɪki dʒæk] *n.,* The Royal Antelope. *Neotragus pygmaeus.* See also **rabbit** and **jack**.

**trouseh**: [tɹausa] "trousers" *n.,* Used rather than "pants". *A shame to weah dis tear-tear trouseh een town.* (I shame to wear this tear-tear trouser in town.) "I'm ashamed to wear these tattered pants in public."

**try**: [tɹaɪ] *v.,* 1. To attempt, to give effort towards something. Because outright refusals are considered rude in Liberia, a common response to a request one does not want to fulfill is "I will try." 2. Used in response to questions about someone's health. Indicates that the person is doing fine. *She trying.* (She trying.) "She's all right."

**tuba**: [tuba] *n.,* A strong drink similar to **hatayee**, but made from local herbs. Common in northwest Liberia.

**tu jai kpono**: [tu jai kpɔnɔ] *n.,* A simple sauce of red oil, meat and onions made by the Vai people. Served when a quick meal is needed for visitors.

**tumba**: [tŭmba] *n.*, A slang term for large and rounded buttocks. Considered very attractive in Liberia. See also **bunga**.

**tycoon**: [taɪkŭ] *n.*, A money-man. A rich person. Slang. *Ma man Joe da real tycoon.* (My man Joe that real tycoon.) "My friend Joe is a rich guy."

# U

**ugly**: [ʌkli] *adj.* Used in a broader sense than Standard English to mean undesirable, unappealing, gross, in poor condition, etc. *Da freen show wa looking too ugly to me.* (That film show was looking too ugly to me.) "I think that movie was awful."

**ULIMO**: [julimo] *n.*, The United Liberation Movement of Liberia for Democracy was a rebel faction during the civil war, opposed to Charles Taylor's NPFL. Because of internal division, the group split into two factions: ULIMO-J, led by General Roosevelt Johnson and made of up mostly of ethnic Krahns, and ULIMO-K led by Alhaji Kromah and made up of Mandingos.

**uncu**: [ʌ̃ku] "uncle" *n.*, 1. While this word can be used to refer to one's parent's brother, it is most often used as a term of respect. 2. In the history of the settling of the various ethnic groups of Liberia, certain groups developed a host/stranger relationship. The tribe who settled an area first became known as the "uncles" to other groups who arrived later. For example, the Kissi are considered "uncles" to the Lorma and several other ethnic groups of Lofa County. Thus, when a person from one of these tribes addresses a Kissi man, they may refer to him as "uncle."

**upcountry**: [ʌkɔ̃tʃɹi] "upcountry" *n.*, The interior regions of Liberia, away from the more developed coastal area. Also known as the **interior** and in past times the **hinterland**.

**upland rice**: [ʌp læ raɪs] *n.*, A variety of rice grown on dry ground, usually in patches of forest cleared through slash and burn agriculture. As opposed to **swam rice**.

**upriwa**: [ʌp ɹɪwa] "up-river" *adj.*, A reference to the Americo-Liberian and Congo people who settled in towns along a major river, away from the coast. Some of these towns include Clay-Ashland, Arthington and Millsburg.

**upstair building**: [ʌp ste bɪdĩ] *n.*, A structure with multiple stories. *De white man live to da upstair building so.* (The white man lives to da upstair building so.) "The white man lives in the multi-story building over there."

# V

**Vai:** [vaɪ] *n,* A prominent ethnic group native to Grand Cape Mount County in western Liberia. Population is approximately 105,000. The Vai speak a Northern-Mande language and were the first language group in sub-Saharan Africa to develop their own script in the early 1800s. The Vai are predominately Muslim with a small Christian presence.

**Vai shirt:** [vaɪ ʃaɪt'] *n.,* A popular style of tailored shirt for men, which originated among the Vai people.

**vex:** [vɛs] 1. *v.,* To anger. *Tek tam befo yu vex de ole ma.* (Take time before you vex the old ma.) "Be careful that you don't make mother mad." 2 *adj.,* To be angry. *Noai vex de way hur fren mean hur so.* (Noai vexed the way her friend meaned her so.) "Noai is angry because of how her friend snubbed her like that."

**video club:** [vidio klʌb] *n.,* A simple theater showing primarily Asian karate films, Nigerian movies, and soccer games. They often consist of merely a small shack with a TV in the front of the room, powered by a generator. *De video club side my hus can cause plenty noise o!* (The video club side my house can cause plenty noise!) "The video club by my house is very noisy!"

**village:** [vɪlɪʒ] *n.,* A residential community, distinguished from a town by its smaller size and lack of a central market.

**vonvon:** [võvõ] *n.,* 1. A finger suspended string spinning toy, often made from the flowers of the **cotton tree.** 2. A flying beetle tied to a string as a children's toy. Usually a green scarab, commonly found around palm wine stands.

# W

**wa** (1): [hwa] "what" *pro.*, A general relative pronoun used rather than that, which, which, who, whom, etc. *Ma man wa to de port cyan call me dee few days.* (My man what to the port can't call me these few days.) "My friend who is at the port hasn't been calling me recently."

**wa** (2): [hwa] "was" or "were" *v.*, Past tense of "be." Not inflected for number as in Standard English. *Musu de woman wa wa to de markeh.* (Musu the woman what was to the market.) "Musu is the woman who was at the market."

**wahala**: [wahala] *n.*, A matter of contention, palaver, fiasco, bruhaha. *Peepo wa toking plenty on de Edwin Snow wahala.* (Peope were talking plenty on the Edwin Snow wahala.) "There was a lot of talk about the Edwin Snow fiasco." See also **halahala**.

**wa happing**: [hwa æpĩ] "what happened" *interrogative.*, Often used in place of "why" in asking a question. *Wa happing yu crying so?* (What happened you crying so?) "Why are you crying like that?"

**wake uh**: [we kʌ] "wake up" *v.*, To awaken or to get up. Does not necessitate a prior state of sleep. It can also mean "Pay attention!" *Wake up pekin befo de dog kesh yu!* (Wake up pekin before the dog catch you!) "Get up kid or the dog is going to get you!"

**wala**: [wala] *n.*, A wooden writing tablet used by Qur'anic students. From the Mandingo language.

**walkabout**: [wakabɔ] *v.*, To stroll, promenade. Often done in the evenings. *A going walkabout een town.* (I going walkabout in town.) "I'm going to stroll around town."

**wan**: [wã] "want" *v.*, 1. Often inanimate objects are said to "want" to do something. For example, rather than saying, "It's looks like it's going to rain," you would say in Liberian English *It want rain.* "It looks like rain is coming." 2. *Wan* is also used to express the idea of almost or nearly. *De banana wan rotten.* (The banana want rotten.) "The bananas are about to get rotten."

**wa nyews**: [hwa ɲus] "what news" *idiom.*, A common way of asking how things are going. Common responses include "No bad," and "I thank God."

**wa play**: [hwa ple] "what place" *interrogative.*, Often used in Liberian English instead of "where" when asking a question. *Da wa play he going so?* (That what place he going so?) "Where is he going like that?"

**wa tam**: [hwa tam] "what time" *interrogative.*, Often used rather than "when." *Wa tam yor going witness show?* (What time y'all going witness show?) "When are you all going to go see a show?"

**wa ting**: [hwa fi] "what thing" *interrogative.*, What. *Da wa ting?* (That what thing?) What is that?"

**wa ting mek ih**: [hwa fi mek ɪ] "what thing make it" *interrogative.*, Why. *Wa ting mek ih yu come soon?* (What thing make it you come soon?) "Why did you come early?"

**wase**: [wes] "waste" *v.*, To spill, pour. Used differently than in Standard English, in that it does not imply a sense of loss. *De rice fini wasing all on de floor.* (The rice finish wasting all on the floor.) 'The rice spilled all over the floor."

**wata**: [wata] "water" *n.*, 1. A river, lake, pond or other body of water. *Dey geh one big wata deh.* (They get one big water there.) 'There is a big body of water there." 2. Any potable liquid. *De baby wan drin teteh wata.* (The baby want drink teteh water.) "The baby wants to drink breast milk."

**wata cow**: [wata kau] "water cow" *n.*, 1. The West African Manatee. *Trichechus senegalensis.* A large aquatic mammal that is very rare and reclusive, but can occasionally be found near the mouths of Liberia's major river systems. 2. The Pygmy hippopotamus *Hexaprotodon liberiensis.* A much smaller and reclusive variety of hippo found only in the deep forest of Liberia and surrounding countries.

**wata deer**: [wata dija] *n.*, The Water Chevrotain. *Hyemoschus aquaticus.* A small, deer-like animal with a reddish-brown coat and white markings. It lives primarily near rivers and creeks where it forages along the banks for food at night.

**wata greens**: [wata gɹis] "water greens." *n.*, A small edible plant with shiny leaves. Used to make a sauce that is served over rice.

**watapolice**: [watapolis] "water police" *n.*, A loose women, a prostitute. *Ain yu see da watapolice passing so?* (Ain't you see that water police passing so?) "Don't you see that prostitute walking by over there?"

**wataside**: [watasaɪ] "waterside" *n.*, 1. A river bank. *We wa to de wataside teking baf de tam we see snek.* (We were to the waterside taking bath the time we saw snake.) "We were at the river bank bathing when we saw a snake." 2. A large market area in downtown Monrovia.

**watchman**: [waʃmɛ̃] *n.*, 1. Night guard. *A ain lek de way de watchman dem can be sleeping so.* (I ain't like the way the watchman them can be sleeping so.) "I don't like how the night watchmen sleep on the job like that."

2. A fishing bobber *Ma man, fish jiking yo watchman.* (My man, fish jerking your watchman.) "Buddy, a fish is pulling on your bobber."

**wawa**: [wawa] *n.,* The light-weight, white wood of the *Triplochiton scleroxylon* tree. Known as "obeche" in the American timber industry. Favored in building construction. *Dey mek de bridge fron wawa. Ih won staylong.* (They make the bridge from wawa. It won't stay long.) "They made that bridge from wawa. It won't last."

**way**: [we] *adj.,* 1. All the way. Used to emphasize distance. *A look fo Peter to de hus, buh A ain see heen deh. Den A budduh wif heen way Reh Li.* (I look for Peter to the house, but I ain't see him there. Then I butt up with him way Red Light.) "I checked for Peter at his house, but I didn't see him there. Then I ran into him all the way in Red Light." 2. Near, in the vicinity of. *A woking Mamba Point way.* (I working Mamba Point way.) "I am working near Mamba Point." 3. A person's manner or personality. *Saye way too rough.* (Saye way too rough.) "Saye has a harsh manner."

**waya**: [weja] *n.,* A popular dance move. Performed by bending the knees and moving them together and apart.

**wayo**: [wejo] *n.,* A prostitute. *De wayo dem plenty on dis street ah night.* (The wayo them plenty on this street at night.) "The prostitutes are all over this street at night."

**weak**: [wik˙] *adj.,* 1. Unmotivated, reluctant. *Da dis plenty corruption bisneh wa mek ih so A weak to pay taxes.* (That this plenty corruption business what make it so I weak to pay taxes.) "It's all that corruption that makes me unmotivated to pay taxes." 2. Small, insignificant. May be used to deflect praise from one's self. *A can try to help Johnson wif hih school fees een my own weak way.* (I can try to help Johnson with his school fees in my own weak way.) "I try to help Johnson with his tuition in whatever way I can, however small."

**well**: [wɛ] *n.,* An open water well. Contrasted with a pump.

**wen off**: [wẽ ɔf] "went off" *v.,* 1. To faint, go into a seizure. 2. To go crazy, lose one's mind. *De zoe chunk medicine on hur an she wen off.* (The zoe chunk medicine on her and she went off.) "The zoe cast a spell on her and she lost her mind."

**wheel**: [hwi] *n.,* A wheelbarrow, or any small wheeled machine. *A wan borrow yo wheel to haul san.* (I want borrow you wheel to haul sand.) "I want to borrow your wheelbarrow to haul sand."

**whip**: [hwɪp] *v.,* To cut grass with a whipper. *A sen Junior to go whip de yar.* (I sent Junior to go whip the yard.) "I sent Junior to go cut the grass."

**whipper:** [hwɪpɔ] *n.,* A long, thin machete with a bent end. Used to cut grass. *Yu muh plea bring de whipper fron eenside de hus, yah?* (You must please bring the whipper from inside the house, you hear?) "Could you please bring the whipper from inside the house?" Also called **chopier.**

**white deer:** [wɛ dija] *n.,* Jentink's duiker. *Cephalophus jentinki.* A light colored forest antelope.

**white heart:** [wɛ haːtʼ] "white heart" *n.,* White symbolizes pure intentions. *We wan gii you dis chicken an kola to show awa white heart fo yu.* (We want give you this chicken and kola to show our white heart for you.) "We want to give you this chicken and these kola nuts to show our pure intentions towards you."

**whop:** [hwap] *n.,* A kind of dance similar to the **waya.**

**wif speed:** [wɪf spi] "with speed" *adv.,* Very fast. *He wa running wif spee on de cycle.* (He was running with speed on the cycle.) "He was going very fast on the bicycle."

**wiki:** [wiki] "wicked" *adj.,* Used rather than evil, cruel, malevolent, thoughtless etc. *Da wiki man spoil hih fren garden.* (That wicked man spoil his friend garden.) "That cruel man destroyed his neighbor's garden."

**win:** [wĩ] *v.,* Used rather than "beat" to indicate victory. *De team fron Nimba win uh.* (The team from Nimba win us.) "The team from Nimba beat us."

**witch:** [wiʃ] "Witch" 1. *n.,* Not usually used in reference to an individual who practices the occultic arts as in Standard English. Rather, it is a spirit that can possess a person. It is believed this spirit can operate independently of the body, leaving the body at night to harm people by the destruction of property or the consumption of their souls. *De sancutta say my aunty geh witch.* (The sandcutter say my aunty get witch.) "The sandcutter said my aunt has a witch." 2. *v.,* A hex or curse which harnesses the power of the "witch." *Dey go up de mountain to mek witch.* (They to up the mountain to make witch.) "They went up the mountain to prepare a curse." 3. *v.,* To place a curse on someone. *Yu wan so de zoe muh witch hur?* (You want so the zoe must witch her?) Do you want the zoe to put a curse on her?"

**witness:** [wɪnɛs] *v.,* Used rather than watch, observe, see, etc. *A witness one fine freen show to my fren hus las night.* (I witness one fine film show to my friend house last night.) "I saw a great movie at my friend's house last night."

**woking**: [wakī] *n.*, Food. Slang usage. *Ma, keep de balance woking.* (Ma, keep the balance woking.) "Mother, keep the remaining food."

**wolum**: [wʌɾʌ̃] "worm" *n.*, Worm—intestinal or earthworms. *Da pekin get wolum. Da wa mek ih hih gut big so.* (The pekin got worm. That what make it his gut big so.) "That boy has intestinal worms. That's why his stomach is so big."

**woman**: [wʊmɔ̃] 1. adj., Female. Can be used for humans as well as animals. *Ma woman sheep coming born.* (My woman sheep coming born.) "My ewe will soon give birth." 2. *n.*, A wife or female sexual partner. *Me and my woman can be to de farm hoday driving boid.* (Me and my woman can be to the farm whole day driving birds.) "My wife and I are always at the farm chasing birds from the rice."

**woman bush**: [wʊmɔ̃ buɪʃ] *n.*, See **sande.**

**woman/man bisneh**: [wʊmɔ̃ bɪnɪ] *n.*, A euphemism for sexual intercourse. *Wen yu na run behine woman bisneh, all dee bad bad sickness cyan kesh yu.* (When you not run behind woman business, all the bad bad sickness can't catch you.) "If you don't sleep around with a lot of women, you won't catch any STDs."

**woman medicine**: [womẽ mɛɾasī] *n* See **love medicine.**

**worf**: [wəf] "worth" *adj.*, To have value. *Deh team ain worf.* (The team ain't worth.) "Their team is worthless."

**worlor**: [wɔlɔ] *n.*, See **slippery soup**

**Worl War**: [wɔ wa:] "World War" *n.*, Due to the intensity of the fighting, Liberians use the term "World War" to refer to the last three battles of the civil war, when LURD was attacking Monrovia. For example, "World War Three" refers to a final siege of LURD in the summer of 2003. See also **Hilter War.**

**worwor**: [wɔwɔ] *adj.*, Ugly, worthless. *Don mine da worwor geh.* (Don't mind the worwor girl.) "Don't pay attention to that worthless girl."

**woto**: [woto] *n.*, A stupid person, a fool. Slang. *Yu woto, yu na know noting.* (You woto, you not know nothing.) "You idiot. You don't know anything."

# Y

**yana**: [jana] *n.*, A walking street vender. Named for their cries of *"yah na!"* (Here now!) *De yana boy deh selling cigarette.* (The yana boy there selling cigarette.) "The vender over there is selling cigarettes."

**yeh** (1): [jɛ] "hear" *v.*, To understand, comprehend. *Wen da man toking hih dialect, you can yeh ih?* (When that man talking his dialect, you can hear it?) "When that man is speaking his language, are you able to understand it?"

**yeh** (2): [jɛ] *interj.*, A contraction of "you hear?" Tagged on to the end of questions or imperative statements similar to the way "OK" is used in informal American English. *A wan so yu muh sponsor me, yeh?* (I want so you must sponsor me, you hear?) "I want you to support me (financially), OK?"

**yellow janna**: [jɛlo d͡ʒana] "yellow jaundice" *n.*, Hepatitis. *Ifan yu drink dis cassava snek wata, ih going hep yo yellow janna.* (If you drink this cassava snake water, it going help your yellow jaundice.) "If you drink the broth of a gabon viper, it will help your hepatitis."

**yonda**: [jãda] "yonder" *adv.*, Over there. *Ih da hus on de hill yonda.* (It that house on the hill yonder.) "It's that house on the hill over there."

**yute**: [jutˀ] "youth" *n.*, A term that may be used for anyone under approximately the age of forty. See also **nyoung boy chief.**

# Z

**za**: [za] *n.,* A person in a zombie-like trance.

**zam**: [zam] *n.,* A fool, an idiot, a simpleminded person. *De way Ernest fail da simpo test sho he real zam.* (The way Ernest fail that simple test show he real zam.) "The way Ernest failed that simple test shows that he's a real idiot."

**zamakolo**: [zamakolo] *n.,* An old, generally undesirable man who nevertheless seduces younger women with material goods.

**zepsay**: [zepse] *adj.,* Crazy, illogical, insane. *Wa kinna zepsay queshon yo ma aksing so?* (What kind of zepsay question your ma asking so?) "What kind of crazy question is your mother asking?"

**zinc**: [zī] *n.,* Corrugated tin roofing. *De zinc staylong owa de hus, buh to buy nyew one too dear.* (The zinc stay long over the house, but to buy new one too dear.) "The tin roofing has been on the house a long time, but it is very expensive to buy new ones."

**zip**: [zɪp] *v.,* To take a puff of a cigarette.

**zo**: [zo] *n.,* A traditional priest. Leaders of the Poro and Sande. Their power often extends beyond the religious to the political realm. *Wa de zoe say, no one can say noting agains ih.* (What the zoe say, no one can say nothing against it.) "No one can say anything against what the zoe says."

**zokolo**: [zokolo] *n.,* A type of edible grub. Used by the **Mano** and **Gio** tribes to make **slippery sauce**.

**zowo**: [zowo] *n.,* A trickster, conman. *Da zowo man play katakata on me an carry all my mar.* (That zowo man play katakata on me and carried all my mar.) "That conman tricked me and took all my money."

**zoot**: [zutˀ] *v.,* To dress up, wear stylish clothes. *Ophelia rally zootin today!* (Ophelia really zooting today!) "Ophelia is really dressing fancy today!" See also **bluff**.

# Liberian Proverbs

Many African cultures prefer indirect means of communication. This can be seen in the extensive use of outside mediators in personal conflict as well as through the use of proverbs. In the African mind, the speech of a refined person is marked by proverbs that can indirectly address any number of serious topics. Liberians have numerous proverbs, called "parables." Below are a few common parables with their meanings.

---

When someone is washing your back, you should wash your stomach. *When someone is helping you, you should also help yourself.*

Baby deer show its mother the trap. *Even an inexperienced person may have something to offer.*

Don't eat crab with shame. *If you decide to do something, do it with gusto.*

Airplane don't blow horn. *If you are not ready, we will leave without you.*

White teeth, black heart. *A smiling face can hide evil intentions.*

Town trap not for rat alone. *Some actions have negative consequences for people other than those for whom they are intended.*

Monkey can't leave his black hands behind. *A person can't hide from their true nature.*

Hurry hurry bust trouser. *Haste makes waste.*

Empty bag can't stand. *It is hard for a hungry person to work.*

Monkey work baboon draw. *Someone benefits from another's work.*

Softly-softly catch a monkey. *Patience is necessary when you are trying to accomplish a hard task.*

Monkey jam eat pepper. *In a tough situation, you are forced to do things you wouldn't usually do.*

Fanti man never say his fish rotten. *A person will not tell you anything negative about the product he is selling.*

The leaf that sweet in goat mouth will run his belly. *Things that are enjoyable now may have bad consequences later.*

# Bibliography

Cansdale, G. S. Animals of West Africa. London: Longmans, 1946

d'Avezedo, Warren L. Some Terms from Liberian Speech. Revised and Enlarged by Michael Even Gold, 1997. Cornell University

Gordon, Raymond G., Jr. (ed.), 2005. Ethnologue: Languages of the World, Fifteenth edition. Dallas, Tex.: SIL International. Online version: http://www.ethnologue.com/.

Hancock, Ian F. "English in Liberia." American Speech, Vol. 49, No. 3/4 (Autumn - Winter, 1974), pp. 224-229

Kortmann et all. A Handbook of Varieties of English A Multimedia Reference Tool. Volume 1: Phonology. Mouton de Gruyter. 2004

Liberiapedia: Liberian Slangs and Idioms. http://www.liberiapedia.com/Liberi-Pedia/Glossary/Entries/2009/ 8/13.htm (Accessed June 29, 2012)

Person, Yves. "Review: Ethnic Movements and Acculturation in Upper Guinea since the Fifteenth Century." African Historical Studies, Vol. 4, No. 3 (1971), pp. 669-689 Published by: Boston University African Studies Center

Sea Breeze Journal of Contemporary Liberian Writings. http://www.liberiaseabreeze.com (Accessed June 29, 2012)

Singer, John. "The Configuration of Liberia's Englishes." World Englishes Vol 16, No 2, pp. 205-231. 1997

Singer, John. An Introduction to Liberian English. Peace Corps/Michigan State University African Studies Center. 1981

Singler, John. "There was fly before dog ear get [a] sore: Vernacular Liberian English vis-à-vis early African American English and still earlier West African Pidgin English." Symposium in honor of David Dwyer, Michigan State University. 2006

If you liked this book, you may also like *Confessions of a Transformed Heart* by Nancy D. Sheppard:

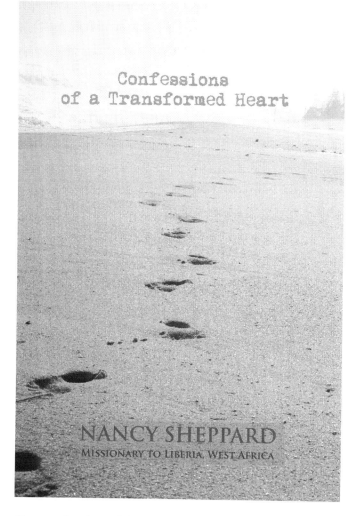

Confessions
of a Transformed Heart

NANCY SHEPPARD
MISSIONARY TO LIBERIA, WEST AFRICA

Nancy Sheppard writes of her experiences during Liberia's devastating civil war with the insight of one who witnessed the tragedy up close. Unable to return to their beloved Liberia after the young family's first term of missionary service, they chose to work among the refugees of the conflict in the neighboring country of the Ivory Coast. But this is not just a war story. This is the story of a woman transformed by the power of God in the midst of hardship.

"Contrary to popular assumption, meaningful work among the impoverished and war torn was not romantic, but was in fact quite the opposite. War refugees were simply people. People ripped from their homes, material goods and every vestige of normal life. Humanity at its rawest—all props gone. All of my props were gone, too. In place of the chipper, Proverbs 31 wife I imagined myself to be was a miserable, depressed, nagging shadow."

Follow the riveting story and see the transformation as God in His jealous love teaches the author about genuine service, submission, freedom, sincere prayer, reverence and humility. Scenarios you can't imagine, yet spiritual lessons with which you can fully identify.

For more information on this book go to
http://www.confessionsofatransformedheart.com

Made in the USA
Lexington, KY
22 December 2013